DEPTH PSYCHOLOGY AND
THE HEALING MINISTRY

DEPTH PSYCHOLOGY
AND THE
HEALING MINISTRY

by
Fred Blum

BOOK PUBLISHERS

One Cranbourne Road, London N10 2BT, England

First published 1990
© Fred Blum

All rights reserved by the publishers
Arthur James Limited
One, Cranbourne Road, London N10 2BT

British Library Cataloguing in Publication Data
Blum, Fred
Depth Psychology and the Healing Ministry
1. Alternative medicine
I. Title
615.6
ISBN 0-85305-302-2

Cover design by The Creative House, Saffron Walden

Typesetting by Stumptype, London

Printed by The Guernsey Press Co. Ltd., Guernsey, Channel Islands

CONTENTS

FRED BLUM

A Tribute from Bishop Stephen Verney

Fred Blum was born in 1914 in Germany. He lived under Hitler's Reich and his Jewish parents died in Auschwitz. Standing in Auschwitz after 1945 he knew that only Jesus the Jew could help him carry that suffering and darkness into light where it could be transformed. It became his life's work.

He escaped to the USA and began work as a sociologist. His PhD thesis was addressed to the change of consciousness which could come to workers in industry through a change in industrial structures. He served with the Senate Committee on Labor Relations, and then under John F Kennedy; in the fifties, with his wife and three children, he worked as a consultant to Scott Bader in Britain to initiate their industrial commonwealth.

It became apparent that a change of structure was not enough, so he turned to Jungian psychology and to the Society of Friends. Here he was teaching about the True Self, and about the Inner Light. He saw that for a change of human consciousness this profound transformation of the ego-self into the True Self had to go hand in hand with a transformation of the structures. He was specially drawn to Gandhi and after Gandhi's death spent many months in India interviewing his associates.

On his own inner journey he came to see Jesus not simply as an historical figure, but as the truth prior to the whole universe. This human beings come to know in the mysterious depths of ourselves and each other, of nature and of God. With this recognition there can come alive in us a new consciousness of the "Cosmic Christ". In 1986

Fred was baptised, and a few months later ordained in the Church of England while remaining a Jew.

Over the past decade his work has been concentrated at The Abbey, Sutton Courtenay, the home of the New Era Centre which he founded in the sixties. Here he gathered a community of people seeking to become agents of transformation in their society.

Fred died on January 8, 1990.
His work lives on.

PROLOGUE

Life is a unity. Healing means to re-establish the harmony and oneness of life. The symbols of the tree and water of life express this deeper unity.

We meet them at the very beginning of the Bible:

When God had created earth and heaven . . . God formed a man . . . (and) planted a garden in Eden . . . and in the middle of the garden he set the tree of life . . .
(Genesis 2, 5—9)

At the end of the Bible, in the Book of Revelation, there is again the tree of life:

Then he showed me the river of the water of life, sparkling like crystal, flowing from the throne of God and of the Lamb down the middle of the City's street. On either side of the river stood a tree of life, which yields twelve crops of fruit, and for each month of the year; the leaves of the tree serve for the healing of the nations. (Revelation 22, 1—2)

All the nations—humankind as a whole—are to be healed, and not merely individuals. Such an understanding of healing is also expressed in St. Paul's letter to Titus: "For the grace of God has dawned upon the world with healing for all mankind" (Titus 2, 11). These words express a universal, cosmic understanding of healing as already indicated in the symbol of the tree which is an image of the cosmos, of the *axis mundi,* the world axis. More specifically, the tree symbolizes the threefold structure of the cosmos: it relates heaven and earth and penetrates to a deeper reality of life.

The holistic-universal quality of healing is a major theme of Isaiah's prophecy. Admonishing "the people of Zion who live in Jerusalem . . . (to follow the true) way . . .", Isaiah describes the redeeming-healing action of God in these words:

> *On each high mountain and each lofty hill shall be streams of running water . . . The moon shall shine with a brightness like the sun's, and the sun with seven times his wonted brightness, seven day's light in one, on the day when the Lord binds up the broken limbs of his people and heals their wounds.* (Isaiah 30, 19–26)

Like the tree, *Biblical healing has a threefold meaning: healing of the individual person, of the human community, and of "all nations".* The healing tree of life yields twelve crops a year. The number 12 is a symbol of true relationships among people. If we take twelve balls and have one of them in the centre, the remaining eleven cluster into a sphere in which all twelve touch each other. Eleven or thirteen balls instead of twelve leave gaps. The figure 12 – symbolic of harmony – thus has a direct concrete meaning.

The Old Testament expresses most vividly the meaning of health as *harmony of relationships in the human community.* For Isaiah, justice and health are inseparable (58, 6–8). In Jeremiah the same theme is alive; healing is related to "the fountain of living water" and to "the word of the Lord" (Jeremiah 17, 13–15). In the New Testament the threefold meaning of the tree of life and the understanding of healing are revealed in the tree on which Christ was crucified. In a third century Easter sermon, Hippolytus, Bishop of Rome, talked about the Cross understood as the Tree of Life in these words:

This tree, wide as the heavens itself, has grown up into heaven from the earth. It is an immortal *growth and* towers *between heaven and earth. It is the fulcrum of all things and the place where they are all at rest. It is the foundation of the round world, the Centre of the cosmos. In it all the diversities of our human nature are formed into a unity. It is held together by the invisible nails of the* spirit *so that it may not break loose from the* divine. *It touches the highest summit of heaven and makes the earth firm beneath its foot, and it grasps the middle regions between them with immeasurable arms.*

This sermon on the Cross as the Tree of Life makes the Life, Death and Resurrection of Jesus of Nazareth the central event revealing the essence of the healing ministry of the healing Church. Located at "the centre of the cosmos", the Cross is "the foundation of the round world". The word "round" — long before the planet earth was conceived as round — symbolizes the unity and oneness of a life lived in Christ. In Him "the diversities of our human nature are formed into a unity." In Him mankind is united in oneness. There is perfect balance and unity rooted in the divine spirit. The result is "immortal growth".

The symbolic quality of the tree transcends the three-dimensional character of the space of daily experience. Instead we are opened to a world of inner experience in which depth and height are synonymous. This is why the tree of life has been represented as rooted both above and below. A good example is the Tree of Life of the medieval Jewish mystics, the Kabbalists, who derived the virgin birth and the trinity from the letters of the Hebrew alphabet and who were one of the few living links between Christianity and Judaism in the middle ages. They chose the symbol of the inverted tree, with its roots towards heaven and its branches towards the earth.

As the tree of knowledge the tree is also a symbol of consciousness. Ultimately the tree is a symbol of the soul, of true relatedness to Life, of the true self. The Greek word which was translated as "soul" in the King James translation of the Bible, is, in the *New English Bible,* translated as the "true self" which denotes the essence of health in a Biblical sense.

PREFACE

The essays constituting this book, though originally written at different times, express a common quest: *to find ways of healing which reveal the ultimate unity and harmony of ~~Life~~ as symbolised in the Tree of Life.* An expression of this basic approach is a quest to unite depth psychological insights with the healing power of the Spirit.

All healing has its source in a deeper reality of life which we may experience in different ways but which is ultimately ONE. While fully recognizing that "God has a thousand names", the divine Truth which has the power of transformation and hence of healing, is most alive in the cosmic Christ who is present in all human beings and in the universe.

Centred in that reality, I have become acquainted with different schools of thought in my training as an analytical psychologist and my subsequent work. Acknowledging the contribution which different schools of thought are making to a wholistic understanding of health, I have developed an approach which recognizes the significance of early childhood experiences without espousing a regressive technique to heal early injuries. We can never really go back into the past any more than we can reverse the flux of time in which our lives are embedded. But we may be decisively influenced, even moulded by past experiences and, in this sense, we can live in the past instead of being free to live in the ETERNAL NOW which alone is true life. This NOW includes past, present and future as measured by the clock while opening us to that Life which is rooted in a timeless reality. As we penetrate into this reality we encounter a healing energy which is the source of all transformation. It is this energy which must become free

11

to penetrate our entire being for us to become whole and hence healed.

The meaning of health varies in different cultures and at different stages of the development of humankind. In the Western world a medical concept of health understood as the absence of specific symptoms, and of healing as "disease eradication", is still prevalent today. However, alternative ways of understanding healing and alternative modes of healing are becoming more and more known. The main emphasis is now shifting from isolated symptomology to a concern with the whole person. Ultimately this means a recognition of a deeper unity of the Spirit, of person-hood and of the human community which leads to a quest for wholeness which encompasses the development of our personally unique potentialities and includes a creative relatedness to the society and the wider community of which we are a part.

Such an understanding of health is in harmony with the potentialities which are alive as we enter a new era in the development of consciousness and the corresponding modes of human relatedness. At the same time we go "back" to the universal meaning of "to heal" which is etymologically related to "whole" and "holy", thus denoting a process of transformation of the whole person. The distinction which has been made between "to cure" and "to heal" is meant to highlight the difference between curing a symptom and healing a person. To cure a symptom is a partial remedy. It may be temporary or it may lead to a shift of symptoms if the real cause of the disturbance is not touched. To heal is a very different process. It is concerned with the essence of a situation since the "whole" and the "holy" are attributes of the kind of person we essentially are. They belong, so to speak, to the very core of our being, to our true self. They are part of the integrity of our lives. They also require an integration of theology, psychology, and the social sciences.

It is true that, as human beings, we can only move *towards* wholeness and thus have a sense of wholeness. We can be in the process of becoming whole but we cannot "be" whole. To imagine that we can encompass in our lives the manifold human potentialities is an illusion. It is tantamount to identifying our partiality with a reality which transcends the limitations of human existence. Such an identification is demonic rather than holy.

This recognition in no way minimizes the significance of our quest for wholeness in order to be healed. The importance of our striving for wholeness becomes evident as we consider the opposite condition of a human being divided in himself or herself. We touch here one of the crucial questions of ethics since the questions of health and illness, good and evil, are interrelated. To give an extreme example: the commandant of a concentration camp may have been the good father of a family—as in fact some were. They were not devoid of any goodness—no human being is—but their goodness was strictly compartmentalized and different aspects of their lives were lived by different parts of their psyche. Another example is a situation where a person imposes on others conditions of work which he or she would be reluctant to accept for himself or herself. The industrial revolution offers many examples though they are in no way limited to that epoch in history.

It is not difficult to find examples where behaviour in one situation is quite incompatible with that in others. The society in which we live today fosters the compartmentalization of our lives by dividing them into different, often sharply separated spheres. Our personal or family life, our working life, our social and political life, usually take place

13

in clearly separated spheres, each having an ethic of its own. No wonder schizophrenia is a typical disease of our time! These examples show that the meaning which we give to healing is not only different from that of the cure of symptoms. It is also quite different from being "well-adjusted". To the extent to which society itself is ill, *I am more ill myself the better adjusted to society I am.* To be healed in the sense of having a sense of wholeness signifies, therefore, something essentially different from being adjusted to whatever social conditions may prevail.

Such an approach to healing incorporates as well as transcends Freudian concerns with infantile experiences and Jungian exploration of archetypes. Fully recognizing the value of these insights, they take on a new meaning and are dealt with in ways differing from the traditional ones once we have recognized the primacy and power of the Spirit. Meditative and related practices of various kinds are, as we shall soon see, essential in this respect. Properly understood they are the *alpha* and *omega* of the healing process.

Centred in the Spirit which is recognized as the source of healing welling up from the ground of our being, we can use the insights of different schools without becoming victims of an eclecticism which is not truly rooted. We can become whole in a way which expresses our personal uniqueness and destiny. This is the touchstone of true healing: *to be obedient to the innermost law of our own being and thus free to become who we are essentially meant to be.*

This book is an attempt to elucidate some of the implications of such a wholistic approach to healing. In the first chapter we explore the basic characteristics of the emerging new world view. All human beings grow and develop in time while being related to a timeless reality. Our aware-ness, furthermore, has an element of partiality if we understand wholeness as encompassing *all* the forms of human life appearing and disappearing in the history of humankind. Last but not least, being human we also partake of good and evil, light and shadow.

Essential for an understanding of the new era on whose threshold we are standing is the recognition that every mode of consciousness is ultimately characterized by the extent and the way in which universal potentialities of human development are actualized in specific space-time-bound forms. These modalities vary for different persons as well as in different cultures and stages of history. Yet at any time and in every culture the true core of personhood is formed by our true self which expresses the unique kind of person we essentially are. Whether we speak in the language of the Bible saying that we must lose ourselves for Christ's sake to find our true self or whether we use the same paradoxical language of the Hindu and designate the true self as "the smallest of the smallest and the greatest of the greatest", we are talking about the way in which a universal truth finds expression in the destiny of every human being. We also speak about the essential quality of relatedness to ourselves, to our fellow human beings, to the human community and organized society as well as to nature and the Spirit.

The true self must be clearly distinguished from the social self which expresses the unique constellation of qualities typical of a specific epoch in the development of consciousness and the corresponding social order. Competitiveness, striving for success, are examples of the values dominant in the welfare capitalism prevalent in our own time. In order to understand it in depth, we must explore the essential characteristics of the medieval, the post-medieval and the new eras. The new era is a synthesis of the two preceding epochs, a synthesis which is rooted in a new awareness of the univeral ground of all life. Throughout the ages these two aspects, the universal and the historically-cultural specific, have been intermingled, thus leading to conflict, persecution and wars. The failure to make a clear distinction leads to a pollution of the Source of Life which manifests itself in manifold ways—the illusion of security through suicidal nuclear weapons being an outstanding and alarming example.

To be healthy in the new era presupposes an ability to differentiate clearly between what is truly universal and what is time/history- and culture-bound. To be able to do so we must be rooted in the universal ground of all Life and thus have access to the truth and energy alive in the Source. *This implies a radical transformation of consciousness which is a precondition for wholeness in the new era.*

Realising the interrelationship between personal and social change, we must also apply universal criteria to the development of a healthy society in order to live as healthy persons in a healthy human community. These criteria are implicit in the natural law tradition of the Church which needs to be cleansed of its time-bound ingredients in order to have something vital to contribute to the new era. The quest for the universal, which is the *alpha* and *omega* of our quest for wholeness, culminates in a living awareness of the ultimate oneness and unity of all life, love being the true bond uniting us to the Creation.

Based on these fundamental insights, we explore ways of healing in tune with the quest for holistic health encompassing our manifold relationships to a life centred in the true self. Psychological methods are inadequate to open the way to true selfhood. Mind and body, individual and communal aspects must be interrelated to make us whole. We are exploring in this context three stages in the healing process and the quality of relationship between the person to be healed and the healer which they require.

The main methods of healing range from meditation and contemplative prayer to the activation of the energy centres in our body. An understanding of the language of dreams is vital in this respect while art, music and the healing energy alive in nature have an important contribution to make.

Healing, thus understood, is centred in the universal-cosmic Christ, the ground and source of healing. While remaining within the Judeo-Christian tradition we realize that such an understanding of healing transcends the time- and culture-bound aspects of Christianity, expressing a universal truth and reverence for life which in its inner core and essence is a mystery.

In the chapter on "Depth Psychology and Salvation" we explore the relationship between our personal development and our destiny. We are concerned with the way in which depth psychology can foster salvation and thereby be in touch with a transcending reality.

The significance of depth psychology consists essentially of the help it can give to enable us to move from the realm of the opposites—where giving and receiving are experienced as two contrasting poles—to the realm of the paradox where we receive through giving and are thus able to follow the one who said: "Whoever cares for his own safety is lost, but if a man will let himself be lost for my sake, he will find his true self." (Matthew 16, 25).

17

In order to understand the meaning and implications of the true way of giving and receiving, we consider the significance of the main stages of human development: infancy and childhood, development of our vocation, of our true unique self, transcendence of "self" and living as persons in community and, finally, the stage of fulfilment. Each stage has its own modality of giving and receiving and as we move through life as healthy human beings, *we move from giving through receiving to the maturity of receiving through giving.*

Examples from my clinical experience show how the ability to give can be violated, leading to a sense of being lost if not actually damned rather than being saved. The Spirit may be inhibited if we do not receive the love which we need to grow up healthily. In this case cosmic forces are activated in us creating a need to build walls to protect us. We may thus erect an impenetrable fortress in which we ourselves are imprisoned. Depth psychology can mobilise the energy which makes it possible to pollute the water of life and even cut us off from the Source of Life.

To fulfil such a creative function, the relationship between the therapist and the person to be healed must transcend the "transference counter-transference" relation-ship—which is essentially of a projective nature—and become a trinitarian or "I-Thou" relationship. In such a relatedness, a "third" element, a deeper universal energy becomes effective as a healing force. We may also designate such a relationship as one in which the cosmic-universal Christ bestows a healing grace.

Yet it would be dangerous to confuse or identify depth psychology and salvation. The former may be a hand-maiden for the latter but salvation transcends whatever may happen on this earth. The quest for salvation may take different forms, which we attempt to elucidate with reference to the meaning of participating in the life, death and resurrection of Jesus of Nazareth. However, we must recognize that we are ultimately faced with a mystery transcending human understanding.

In the chapter on "The Healing Church" we explore first the Biblical understanding of healing as being almost synonyimous with salvation. For Isaiah health implies a caring attitude as regards one's fellow human beings. In his prophecies about Jesus's self-sacrifice, healing is understood as a relationship to life which is the result of a living relationship to God. It is indeed true that through renunciation Jesus of Nazareth became a pure channel of the divine power to heal.

Such a wholistic conception of healing is implicit in the Hebrew language which does not separate what we call the spiritual, the psychological and the social-communal. Healing is never a one-way act but takes place in a relationship in which a deeper trust and openness to a divine reality is present. These are essential ingredients of the kind of faith which is a precondition for healing to take place. St. Paul's understanding of the Body of Christ as the "carrier", "prototype" or "image" of the healing ministry of the Church indicates most clearly the goal of healing as well as "containing" the healing power of transformation.

The question arises in this context: What is the relationship of the Body of Christ, the true Church, to the various churches? Since the churches are part of a specific culture at certain stages in the development of consciousness, their witness to health and healing has a time-bound dimension. Living in time as well as in eternity, we, as members of different churches as well as of the Church universal, must live, therefore, in and with a creative tension between our time-bound culture and our being members of the Body of Christ. As we become conscious of this tension we become agents of transformation of what is into what is meant to be.

While each person must follow his or her own personal calling as part of the healing ministry of the Church, a corporate witness based on a shared vision of a true human community is vital for our time. The natural law tradition of the Church expressed in universal principles of true communal and societal relationships is an important bridge to ground our vision in a way which enables us to act upon it.

Non-violence is the best way of acting in harmony with the Biblical tradition. Combined with an open experimental approach it enables us to develop new ways of acting—and living—while remaining organically related to an age-old tradition. Since non-violence is rooted in love rather than hatred, forgiveness and reconciliation are essential aspects of a struggle for true transformation of what is not in harmony with Truth into a human community imbued by the Spirit of the One who could say "I am the Way, I am the Truth and I am life." (John 14, 61).

In the chapter entitled "The Wounded Healer", we explore the nature of a relationship between two people in and through which the transforming energy contained in a deeper reality of life is activated. To be able to enter into such a relationship we ourselves must know in some way what it means to be wounded. Otherwise we cannot under-stand—and hence love—the person to be healed at a depth which makes transformation and therefore healing possible.

At the same time "the wounded healer" and the person with a wound to be healed must touch the deeper reality of life which contains the source of a healing-transforming energy. The process of transformation is usually accompanied by a struggle between "good and evil" within us. We are exploring in this context how an injury suffered in early childhood activates negative forces beyond our control, creating a sense of guilt which may be crippling. To be healed from such injuries we must be able to bear a wound "in God's way" by freeing us from resentment and negative feelings and thus transcending the contradictions of human experience. Our will and the divine grace are thus able to interact.

Will-power and grace, activity and passivity, transformation and acceptance, thrust and receptivity are interrelated and interact when the wounded healer and the person to be healed touch the ground which contains the Source of the transforming power incarnated in Jesus as the Christ. In its deepest meaning, to be the wounded healer means to be able to enter into the mystery of the Passion, and to experience in ourselves that another human being has taken our wounds upon himself or herself to the limit of giving his/her life for us.

The last chapter shows the potentialities of holistic healing centred in meditation, whilst using various approaches ranging from dream interpretations to Laya Yoga. It shows how a deep and early wound is in the process of being healed in and through a twofold relationship: to a deeper reality of life — to the Source, activated through a personal relationship which transcends the transference relationship between the healer and the person who seeks healing. Highlights of the healing process are the moments when the divine presence is coming alive spontaneously — as well as being mediated through a human encounter at depth.

We show how the deprivation of love and light in

infancy and early childhood caused profound pain and suffering, summed up in a drawing of "a baby living in solitude". The fears and despair aroused by such cosmic loneliness and abandonment was accompanied by the arousal of powerful negative emotions which are automatically aroused in the helpless infant or child. Though feeling paralysed, trapped and blocked, the person to be healed could nevertheless remain open enough to a living relationship with the immanent as well as with the transpersonal Spiritual Centre alive for her in Jesus. This enabled her to face her pain and suffering in a creative way and without resentment while going through "the dark night of the soul" towards the divine light. This process which combined what she described as "slow cooking" with an experience of grace, may best be understood as an encounter with a transforming fire kindled and nourished by a universal reality in which the Source of all true healing is rooted. As she was freed to move on this path of transformation, she could live more wholly and with less interference, the love alive in her deep relationship to Jesus, experiencing a new and more encompassing wholeness.

Chapter 1

HEALTH AND HEALING IN THE NEW ERA

I.

To be human means to be in a constant process of becoming. Only God can say "I am; that is who I am." (Exodus 3, 14). A human being can only say "I am realizing my true being through becoming." We partake of a process of growth and development both as individual people and as members of a given society and culture. We are born, go through infancy, childhood and adolescence to a maturity which culminates in death, the gateway to a new life. As members of a given culture we may have been born in the stone age, we may have been the child of a Roman soldier, or of a medieval craftsman. We may have been born into the Renaissance, the Enlightenment, the world of the 19th century or we may be living now in the 20th century as it moves towards its end. Whatever may have been the case, we are alive at a certain stage of the evolutionary process as well as in a specific culture or civilization which determines a range within which our potentialities can be developed.

To partake in this twofold process of personal development and historical-cultural evolution means that our awareness is bound to be partial. The human condition is indeed characterized by a kind of partiality which gives to the quest for wholeness a particular meaning and significance, "for our knowledge and our prophecy alike are partial" (1 Cor. 13, 9). We have a limited life span and we have limited potentialities. We are, furthermore, conditioned by the culture and civilization into which we are born. We can have but glimpses of the ultimate unity of

23

all life. Yet our experience of wholeness can be alive and real because we are not only "becoming". We "are" also alive in the eternal now. Thus "to be" means to transcend clock-time and have a living relationship to a universal timeless reality of life. To be/become thus defines the very essence of our humanity.

A final characteristic of the human condition is our being involved in a struggle between good and evil. There is light and darkness in us. To be human means to encounter these opposites, to bring them somehow into a balance and/or to transcend them. Ultimately this means a movement from the realm of the opposites into the deeper realm of the paradox. In the former the light may be extinguished, in the latter "the light shines on in the dark, and the darkness has never mastered it." (John 1, 5). Though present, darkness can no longer dominate us once we have passed the threshold of the paradox in our personal development.

These four fundamental characteristics: *relatedness to a timeless reality of life, development in time, partiality of awareness and partaking of good and evil* are the existential reality to which our criteria of healthy growth and development must be related. At first they may seem to make the quest for wholeness an illusory one. But this is not the case, provided we are centred in our true self.

II

The true self expresses the kind of persons we essentially are, that is the kind of persons we are meant to become as we grow and develop our personal gifts and potentialities. All human growth and development takes place in relationship: to our-selves, to our fellow human beings, to the human community and organized society, to nature and to a deeper reality of life. These relationships do not constitute five separate isolated realms of life but form an interacting unity. The way we relate to other people is interrelated with the way we relate to our own centre as well as with the values of the culture to which we belong. The extent to which a given culture or civilization affects us is, in turn, greatly influenced by the depth of our rootedness in a deeper reality of life and by the way in which the latter interacts with the culture of which we are a part.

The true self thus understood is a multidimensional unity which links us to the various spheres or realms constituting our life-space. These spheres may be designated as the spatial dimensions to be distinguished from, yet interrelated with, the two time dimensions mentioned above: history and a timeless reality transcending history. Our relationship to our life-space is always two-fold: as a time-bound space and as time-less space. We are, therefore, always standing in a dialectic relationship to life: in us the time-bound, historically and culturally unique and the time-less interact. They are inter-woven, bound together in our body in which the spirit is incarnated.

The way in which space-time and eternity manifest themselves in any particular person determines the way in which the potentialities of the unique human being "I" essentially am, may unfold. "I" live at a particular moment in history and "I" am related to a universal reality which follows a lawfulness different from the historical process though it interacts with the laws of history. "I", furthermore, have a law of my own true being. To follow this law and thus to be true-self centred, we must be able to transcend the time-bound historically and culturally unique aspects of life and be/become nourished by a universal reality and truth. When these conditions are fulfilled we are healthy—having our being in and moving towards wholeness.

The five "spatial" dimensions of the true self, the time dimension and the timeless-universal reality, interact and constitute the world in which we move and have our being. Health understood as wholeness encompasses these seven dimensions or aspects of life. We are healthy if we are on the way to a wholeness which expresses our essential uniqueness in a living relationship to the seven aspects of life just mentioned. To be more specific: *We are healthy (1) if we are rooted in the time-less reality, open to the Source of all life and hence have a living relationship to the ultimate unity and wholeness of life; (2) if through this relationship we are centred in such a way as to be free to grow and to participate in the process of Creation by developing our personal uniqueness and (3) if we are in a creative-transcending relationship to the world in which we are living, free to be agents of transformation of what "is" into what is meant to be.*

In the language of depth psychology, the true self is our unique and essential centre as distinguished from that centre which is formed by the ego or little self. To be human means to share those qualities which are peculiarly human inasmuch as they distinguish a human being "in essence" from an animal or from an angel. These qualities are at the same time universally human inasmuch as all human beings have these qualities as potentialities of development. The uniqueness of the true self and its universality are indivisible because in each person these human universals are combined in a unique way, each potential being alive in a different intensity and in a different form. To develop our true self means to unite

our peculiarity and universality by developing our uniqueness in a living relationship to other people, to the human
community and society, to nature and to a deeper reality
of life. Thus understood, the true self is a unique combination of universally shared needs and potentialities. In this
sense every human being is unique, yet the "building
stones" of our uniqueness are universal.

In biblical language the true self is our essence, our soul.
It is interesting that the Greek word *psyche* which was
translated in the King James version of the Bible as "soul"
is translated in the New English version as "true self".

> *Jesus said to his disciples: "If anyone wishes to be a*
> *follower of mine, he must leave self behind: he must*
> *take up his cross and come with me. Whoever cares for*
> *his own safety is lost; but if a man will let himself be*
> *lost for my sake, he will find his true self. What will a*
> *man gain by winning the whole world at the cost of his*
> *true self? Or what can he give that will buy back that*
> *self?"* (Matthew 16, 24—26)

These words are paradoxical: to lose in order to find,
to receive by giving. For such an admonition to be meaningful, we must first have gained what we are asked to
lose. We cannot lose something that we do not possess.
We must first develop a strong "I" and be on our way to
true-self-realization before we can take up our cross and
follow Him. Until these conditions have been fulfilled,
we move in the realm of the opposites in which we cannot
find anything by losing. We must have reached the stage
of development where we can move into the realm of the
paradox before we can find our true self by losing all
those tendencies and qualities which are ego-centred rather
than true-self centred.

The way in which the call to lose ourselves was understood in the Victorian era and still often is today, was tragic because it led to stunted rather than to fulfilled lives, the opposite of what it was intended to be. The roots of this tragedy lie in a conception of "egoism" and "altruism" which failed to distinguish between the true self and the little self and which kept the understanding of selfhood within the realm of the opposites. As a result it considered a concern with one's own development in opposition to a concern for others. It was an either-or attitude rather than a giving-and-receiving experience — a paradox which was already expressed in the Biblical injunction: "Love your neighbour as yourself." (Matth. 22, 38). We must love ourselves by truly responding to the call to develop our God-given potentialities in order to become the kind of person whom we are meant to be. This is the foundation for a self-giving love through which we receive more than we give rather than losing by giving. Giving "from the overflow of our heart" enriches us while it enriches others. Love thus understood is the hallmark of our true humanity — the ultimate test of health.

In Eastern religion the true self is defined as "the smallest of the smallest and the largest of the largest." Such an understanding is reflected in Jesus' comparison of the mustard seed and the kingdom of God (Jesus, after all, was an Easterner): "As a seed, mustard is smaller than any other; but when it has grown it is bigger than any garden plant; it becomes a tree, big enough for the birds to come and roost among its branches." The mustard seed is also the symbol of a transforming faith. "If you have faith no bigger than a mustard seed, you will say to this mountain, 'Move from here to there!' and it will move; nothing will prove impossible for you." The mustard seed, symbol of the true self, is thus the symbol of the transforming power as well as of the Kingdom in which the

Body of Christ comes to its timeless fulfillment.

The biblical, depth-psychological and Eastern understanding of the Self are unique expressions of the same reality: the innermost core, the true Centre of all Life. If we are centred in our true self we are also centred in Christ because our true self is related to—indeed it is part of—the Centre of the universe and hence the Centre at and through which Christ enters ourselves.

III.

To understand the implications of true-self centredness as the essence of health it is important to compare it with our social self. The latter expresses all those attitudes and values which are typical for the society and culture of which we are part. If competitiveness is an important aspect of our culture, the social self has a competitive component. If success is important for gaining social esteem, the striving for success will be part of the social self. Veblen's "conspicuous consumption" is a good example of attitudes typical of the social self.

The specific expression of the social self depends upon the stage reached in the development of consciousness as well as upon the unique selection of human potentialities which accounts for the difference in the patterns of culture. Starting from an original oneness which is relatively undifferentiated, development for humankind as a whole and for individual people signifies differentiation of a relatively inchoate unformed reality into a pattern which has a centre and varied forms grouped around it. Whatever is differentiated needs to be integrated to create an inter-dependant and inter-acting unity. World views and historical epochs vary basically as regards the nature of the differentiation—each forming a different pattern—and the way in which the various parts are brought into unity.

Looking at the Western world in such a perspective we can distinguish three major periods: the medieval, (about 1000—1500), the post-medieval (1500—the present), and the new era, at whose threshold we are standing. Table I shows the unique constellation of universal potentialities "chosen" in the process of differentiation and integration. The left-hand column shows what constituted "reality" for medieval man and the right-hand column indicates what aspects post-medieval man experienced as "real".

The medieval world was centred in the Spirit—as most concretely manifested in the medieval Cathedral. At the centre of medieval man's awareness was the symbol which related him to a deeper reality of life. Medieval man lived

TABLE I

Medieval Mode of Consciousness	Postmedieval Mode of Consciousness
symbol	sign
substance	form
quality	quantity
emotion	thought
subject	object
inner	outer
spirit	matter
soul	psyche
group	individual
values	facts
faith	science
absolute	relative

in an inner-directed world of faith in which the absolute was experienced strongly. He was embedded in a hierarchical order which gave him a definite place in society. His emotions were powerful and difficult to master because they were relatively little differentiated.

The post-medieval world was in all essentials the opposite of the medieval world. The sign replaced the symbol as the basic indicator of reality. This signified a shift from the primacy of a deeper reality of life (which we can only grasp symbolically) to a reality whose essence we understand through the sign language of mathematics. Post-medieval man developed primarily his rational potentialities. He gave to his emotions a secondary place. Hence the language of mathematics had a "formal" quality as distinguished from the substantive reality of values and emotions. Post-medieval science strove to be purely factual, "free from value judgments". It was concerned with outer objects rather than with inner happenings. Its philosophical counterpart was "cultural relativism" rather than transcendental absolutism. Its methodology emphasized quantitative measurements rather than qualitative evaluations. Thomas Aquinas' *Summa Theologica* was of a very different nature. Its logic was that of symbolic associations and inner substantive relationships.

A comparison of the right and left hand columns in the Table above clearly illustrates the fundamental shift in the experience of life due to different ways of "seeing", that is, selecting and differentiating. The reality known in the post-medieval world was experienced as exclusive of if not opposed to the medieval world view. The new era, however, synthesises the universal truths underlying the world views of the medieval and the post-medieval epochs. The truly new is not the result of a reaction against what "is" — though such reactive processes are difficult to avoid at a

31

time of transition. Nor is the new compatible with a romantic longing for a time which in its historically unique expression belongs to the past. Essentially the "new" is a recognition of the universal truth of the medieval eras which have to be united in new forms and ways.

The achievement of such a unity requires a fundamental transformation of consciousness. Hitherto neglected and perhaps deeply repressed aspects of life must be re-discovered while new insights are being incorporated into our world view. It is not always easy to maintain a proper balance in such a process. We must be particularly on guard against the danger of compensating for the one-sideness of the post-medieval world view by the one-sideness of an opposite world view. We must fully accept the true achievements of the last five hundred years of Western history by discovering their universal truth which is alive at their core, no matter what historically unique—and outmoded—expressions the universal core-truth may have taken. The rational world of outer objects and mathematical sign language is a real world though we can recognize it today as being a partial reality only, while preserving its essential truth (which is universal) and incorporating it into a more wholistic world view.

However, the nature of the new era whose dawn we are witnessing can not be adequately understood by the transformation due to a new synthesis of essential dimensions of the medieval and post-medieval world views. Not only the latter is coming to an end—the whole patriarchical world view which dominated the Western world for thousands rather than for hundreds of years is also coming to an end. This means a radical reevaluation of the significance of the feminine which has a much more central place in the newly emerging consciousness than it had in the past.

IV.

Holistic therapy must be aware of the existential situation in which we find ourselves today in the Western world and which affects the whole planet earth. To become whole at such a moment in history—when we witness fundamental transformations of consciousness—makes it imperative to transcend the mode of consciousness alive in the social self that is typical of our time. This is a precondition for an expansion of consciousness opening us to a more comprehensive world view incorporating the potentialities of the new era which we are called to bring to fruition.

To be able to realize these potentialities we must be rooted in and nourished by the universal order with which we have already become familiar as the ground of all being and becoming. Containing the Source of all life, the water of life which nourishes us with the very essence of life—the universal is permeated by an energy which has the power of transformation. All healthy growth and development is contingent upon openness to this Source, upon access to the water of life.

There are many reasons why there may be blocks in our way, the most hurtful ones being the need to cut ourselves off from this Source in order to defend ourselves against the onslaught of negative forces activated through lack of true affirmation in infancy and childhood. Even if we do not have to overcome such obstacles, partaking of the human condition means that there is a constant need to cleanse, to purify the water of life. It does not flow automatically as pure water. Its flow is affected by the impact of the opposites which may cut us off from this Source and affect our ability to see people and situations as they really are. The more our vision and experience

33

are vitiated by identifications, by projections, and by the intermingling of universal and personally, historically and culturally unique aspects, the more the water of life becomes polluted. When the water of life is channelled in such a way that it enhances the opposites and leads to a division of the world into black and white, rather than enabling us to overcome divisions and separations, its energy may even become demonic. This inhibits our struggle against evil and causes ill-health.

While these predicaments are part of the human situation, a special challenge arises at a time of fundamental transformation of consciousness, that is the challenge to partake in the development of a new world view while freeing us from a world view which was dominant for centuries and which moulded every fibre of our being. Ultimately this newness is due to an awakening of universal potentialities which were hitherto dormant in the Source of all life. To actualize these potentialities we must be able to differentiate between what is truly universal in the presently prevailing mode of consciousness and the corresponding societal and ecclesiastical institutions, and what belongs to the post-medieval era which is now coming to an end. Granted that although all great religions and world views strove for universality or claimed to have found an absolute truth, they were in fact — and still are — a mixture of timeless, universally true insights and of historically as well as culturally time-bound ideas and concepts. The result of such con-fusion has been separations and conflicts incompatible with true centredness in the Spirit.

Recent psychological and sociological insights enable us to differentiate between what is universal and what is conditioned by the particular culture into which we are born and whose basic attitudes and values form our social self. As we have seen in the preceding explorations, the "building stones" of our personalities are universal, yet they take a unique form in every human being depending upon our personal uniqueness, the stage in the development of consciousness in which we participate and the historical and cultural circumstances in which we live. These factors operate like energies affecting the stream of consciousness. They intermingle in this stream in a way which may give to personally, culturally or historically unique phenomena, ideas or attitudes, the sanction of a universal truth.

To live in the spirit of the new era we must be able to differentiate between the energies and values related to our *true* selves, our *little* selves and our *social* selves. The ability to do so constitutes the key to the quest for universality and wholeness which is the foundation of health in the new era. Though an awareness of the need for such a differentiation has been alive in many civilizations, the ability to actualize it has only existed exceptionally. In the Judeo-Christian tradition the need to differentiate between the "word of God" and "the precepts of man" has been clearly recognized, yet it has only exceptionally permeated the consciousness of the faithful. More often than not, culture—and history-bound truths—have been identified with an absolute truth.

The result of such identifications was the sanctification of whatever order existed by endowing historically unique attitudes as well as social institutions with universal meaning and validity. Examples are the sanctification of the power of kings and emperors during the middle ages and more recently the identification of capitalism with free markets and a free society ruled by the invisible hand of God.

Looking back into history, it is relatively easy to see

that a person who persecuted others as heretics or as "witches", experiencing them as the incarnation of evil, was not a balanced, healthy person. It is equally easy to realise that the justification of slavery as corresponding to a peculiarity of human nature which creates superior and inferior human beings was a rationalization of a class position rather than a universally true insight into human nature. It is more difficult to realize that the organization of work typical of our time is based on a division of people into two groups, those who are creative—and so need creative work opportunities—and those who are not—and so may languish in an organization which prostitutes them and means performing meaningless tasks eight hours a day, five days a week, fifty-two weeks a year—maybe for a life-time. It may be even more difficult to become aware that the experience of security through nuclear weapons and the concomitant belief that an instrument of suicide could be an effective deterrent is a manifestation of ill-health and insanity. What would we say if we should meet somebody who derives his/her sense of security from having an explosive attached to his neighbour's bed which he/she could unleash by pushing a button, knowing that his neighbour also has a button which, if pushed, will unleash explosive attached to his bed? Yet this has been exactly the inter-national situation which gives the illusion of security to millions of people in the Western world.

This is but an extreme illustration of a separation from the universal ground of life. The possibility of this happening is due to a basic aspect of the human condition: the necessity to relate the universal to a unique, time-bound mode of consciousness. This does not pose any problems as long as we can differentiate between what is universal and what is time-bound, thus enabling the universal energies to be expressed in ever new forms and ways. But if we are not open to the power of renewal inherent in the universal Source, its energy may "congeal" in forms and ways of life which have outlived their true meaning and hence their usefulness. If this happens the forms or ways become rigid and eventually encapsulate the spirit alive in their universal core.

We find many examples of this process in all historical periods. We find idealism betrayed by the way in which human institutions develop. We find reform movements as well as revolutions leading to results very different from those intended. We find codes of morality and ethics losing their true meaning and becoming obstacles rather than guides to human growth and development. The processes underlying all these phenomena constitute a pollution or blockage of the Source of life. The only way to avoid this is to develop a mode of consciousness which enables us to penetrate to the universal Source as well as to differentiate between the universal core of all life and the unique form —or rather forms—which it has taken. The ability to discern this is a precondition for having access to the truth alive in the Source of life.

The differentiation between a universal truth and the time-bound ways amounts to a radical transformation of consciousness. Instead of being primarily members of a certain culture (because we are centred in our social self), we will become primarily human beings (because we are centred in our true self). This will enable us to become integrated in such a way that we have a living awareness and relationship to humankind as a whole. To be healthy in the new era means to be sufficiently free of projections, inner divisions and false identifications, to have a living sense of oneness with all human beings.

Such an understanding of health has far-reaching implications for our relationship to the society and culture into which we were born and in whose institutions we are embedded. Until now most people have participated in their social institutions in terms of their social rather than their true selves. Unable to differentiate between the cultural and historical uniqueness and the universal foundation of their society, they have given absolute validity to time-bound doctrines and institutions. They have experienced their society—whether it was the medieval world or a *laissez-faire* market economy—as having a universal, timeless character.

In the absence of an articulated awareness of the nature and manifestation of the universal order, it is indeed unavoidable that its image—which is alive in the depth of all human beings—is projected on the historically and culturally unique social order of which we are part, be it capitalist, socialist or communist. What appeared to post-medieval man as a "scientific" understanding of society— science being an essential expression of the post-medieval world view—is in fact a con-fusion of universal-timeless and time-bound aspects of reality. This confusion is the result of the projection of the image of a universal order onto a particular historically unique system.

The ability to "take back" this projection and to be able to differentiate clearly between these aspects as well as to understand their interaction is a decisive characteristic of the newly emerging consciousness. It is a precondition for moving towards that wholeness which is a potentiality of the new era. We must become conscious of the "image of the universal" alive in us and the particular human and social order which we, as responsible human beings, have helped to create and in whose continual transformation we must participate. The inability to do so accounts not only for wars, persecution and "class" struggles; it also underlies the separation of the great religions—even the separations within Christianity. Whenever a particular doctrine is endowed with a universal truth, destructive conflicts are bound to arise.

To be healthy in the new era a radically different mode of consciousness must develop. Rooted in the universal ground of our being and becoming, we must stand in a creative tension to whatever the institutions of the existing society and culture may be, and become responsibly involved as agents of transformation of what *is* into what *is truly meant to be* in terms of our deepest insight into a universal truth. Such an awareness releases energy for participation in the ongoing process of creation, for a continuous movement towards wholeness, a wholeness which includes social institutions and relates them creatively to our personal lives. Our "inner" world and the "outer" world of the human community, of the society in which we are living, of nature and of an ultimate reality must be seen as an interrelated and interacting reality. We thus transcend the opposition of "inner" and "outer" typical of the post-medieval world view, and participate in a continuous transformation of the social order bringing about an "open" society. All social institutions are in danger of congealing, becoming rigid and closed unless people stand in an open transforming relationship to them.

To be able to perform such a function we must have universal criteria for the development of a healthy society. Such criteria may be found in the insights of natural law alive in the Judeo-Christian tradition. By critically examining the time-bound aspects of the natural law tradition, and by penetrating to its genuinely universal content, we will be able to define criteria which are truly universal and which can be applied in different ways, depending upon specific cultural and historical conditions as well as upon personally unique situations. This is important in order to avoid a new dogmatism and to transform closed systems into open ones. Universality and flexibility are thus combined.

An example of universal criterion for the development of a healthy human community is the natural law postulate that human beings should always stand to each other in a relationship of "ends" rather than "means". To respect another human being I must relate to her or him as an "end", as a person endowed with a uniquely true self. Whenever I use another person as a means, for whatever purposes this may be, I am violating his or her essential humanity. This basic postulate of natural law is enough to build a true foundation for a society radically different from ours in which people often are means for purposes alien to their true selves. As we respond to the existing social institutions in terms of our deepest understanding of the universal principles of natural law—drawing on the wisdom contained in the Source of life as well as on its energy—we become free to enter into a struggle to make our society ever more truly human by ever more truly reflecting the truth of the universal order.

Such an involvement implies a reciprocal interrelationship between individual and social change. As we, individual persons, become transformed we become engaged in transforming society. As society becomes more truly human and more just the individual process of transformation is fostered in turn. The recognition of such an interrelationship makes our freedom to be agents of change in the existing social institutions an important ingredient of being healthy in the new era.

VI.

A transcending-transforming quality of relatedness to life opens the way to an experience of the ultimate openess and unity of all life; to a living awareness that all life, though often divided in itself, is ultimately one. We must penetrate into a deeper reality to be able to experience this unity in spite of the contradiction of daily life.

As we grow into such an awareness we become more deeply related to others and experience more and more consciously the common reality alive in all of us. In this sense we live more with others and others live more in us. We also become more deeply related to the One who could say: "because I live, you too will live; then you will know that I am in my Father, and you in me and I in you." (John 14, 20).

The quality of relatedness which opens us up to such an experience and which in turn is enlivened by it, is love. In it the essence of health is summed up. We are healthy inasmuch as we can truly love. Essentially love is the ability for self-transcendence, for giving ourselves to others without expecting a return. Through love we affirm "the other" while ultimately affirming our true self. Such love

> is patient; love is kind and envies no one. Love is never boastful, nor conceited, nor rude; never selfish, not quick to take offence. Love keeps no score of wrong; does not gloat over other men's sins, but delights in the truth. There is nothing love cannot face; there is no limit to its faith, its hope, and its endurance.
>
> (1 Cor., 13, 4—7).

Love, to be whole in the spirit of the newly emerging consciousness, must encompass all spheres of life and must affirm all of humankind. This does not mean that we could possibly stand in the same personal loving relationship to all people as we can to those closest to us. But it does mean that we are so deeply rooted in the universal ground of life that we recognize "that of God" in every human being. More specifically it means that we take seriously the words "Always treat others as you would like them to treat you: that is the law and the prophets." (Matthew 7, 12). If I do not want to spend my own life with meaningless work—not to speak of lack of any opportunity for work—I cannot accept a situation in which this is the fate of millions of human beings. If I do not want my child to starve, I cannot possibly accept that another human being's child is starving while I am eating my meal. Granted, "I" do not have the power to change the whole world. But I am able to act somehow provided I am centred in my true self and thus related to a deeper, more powerful reality of life. I am free to take a stand if my love has a holistic meaning and is a living reality.

This is the crucial issue: can we create a social order which is in basic harmony with that deeper reality of life which is expressed in a universal order? Or are we condemned to live in a world in which some people find fulfilment by actively partaking of the ongoing creative process while others are condemned to stultifying soul-destroying jobs—or un-employment? Are we endowed with enough insight to use the food we have grown to satisfy human needs or are we so impotent—and so bereft of the divine—that we must destroy food while people are starving to death? To give a positive answer to these questions does not imply a perfect world. It simply implies the conviction that we can create a basically sane world if we are truly related to the Source of Life.

If we are unable to build a true social order, our health is in danger of being at the expense of the ill-health of another person. I must then inflict on "my neighbour" what I do not want to suffer myself. Love in a holistic sense is an illusion in such a world. If, however, we are able to build a social order rooted in a deeper reality of life, the health and love in the holistic sense understood here are realistic possibilities, no matter how imperfect these realizations may be. Such a development is indeed a real potentiality as we enter a new era in the development of human consciousness.

It is important to realize that such an understanding of health in terms of healthy persons living in a healthy human community is not new. It is vividly expressed in the Old Testament concern for justice in general and in particular in the provision of a jubilee year when true social relationships are to be restored. In Christianity it is, as already mentioned, expressed in the tradition of "natural law" which contains the fundamental principles for the organization of society. What is new is our ability to differentiate in a much clearer way between the universal core of all life and its time-bound expression while being fully aware of their interaction. We can thus be truly "in the world but not of the world". We can stand on firm ground while being open to the new potentialities which arise every new day, open to our neighbour wherever he or she may be; open to life. The openness of the new consciousness will enable us to express a universal truth in different modes and world views. To sum up: health in the new era implies the freedom to realize the universal essence in the most diverse cultural and personal ways. It also implies the ability to build a healthy human community and society in which all human beings have the opportunity to partake of healthy growth and development. Finally our understanding of health implies a living relationship to a deeper reality of life as well as to the evolutionary process in which we participate both as individual people and as members of a given society and culture.

VII.

The quest for holistic health thus understood requires a holistic approach to healing. Since no one human being can encompass the various aspects — and methods — necessary to deal with the whole person, a team approach is necessary. While each member of the team contributes different insights and skills the team must share a basic vision. There is room for a wide range of personal experience, understanding and world views within such a team. But the team must share three fundamental tenets: They are:

(1) an understanding of a human being as a unity of body and soul,

(2) a realization that the individual soul-body forms part of a wider body formed by humankind as a whole, and

(3) a knowledge that the body of humankind is interrelated with a deeper reality of life.

What we usually call "psyche" is inadequate for such a holistic approach. The original meaning of psyche in Greek thought is more akin to what we call "soul". We shall, therefore, use the concept of "soul" or, following the new translation of "soul" in the *New English Bible* as "the true self", we shall use the latter as interchangeable with "soul". The true self encompasses as we have seen, not only the psychological mechanisms and the laws of growth and development underlying psychological and societal processes; it also encompasses our relationship to nature as

44

well as the manifestation of a deeper transpersonal reality of life.

The soul thus understood cannot be separated from the body which is but the visible form of our essence — of our true self. The fact that we stand and walk erect on two feet, for example, distinguishes us from all animals and expresses something essential about what it means to be human. The body understood as a visible form is not merely a biological entity but is animated by the soul which penetrates it in its entirety. The body is a manifestation of the Spirit in "the flesh". The bio-spiritual reality of our body must, furthermore, be understood as an organ of a wider body — the body formed by the human community. Whenever we are centred in our true self we are, at the same time, related to humankind and to a deeper reality of life. This unity of the essentially and truly human and of the divine is clearly expressed in the saying of St. Paul: "For Christ is like a single body with its many limbs and organs, which, many as they are, together make up one body . . . whether we are Jews or Greeks, whether slaves or free men . . . That one Holy Spirit was poured out for all of us to drink." (1 Cor. 12, 12—13).

Ultimately, our approach to healing is determined by an understanding of health as a quality of relatedness to life which frees us to experience ourselves as members of one body. The implicit understanding of the unity of the soul and the body, of the embeddedness of every individual soul-body in the body of humankind and of the interrelatedness of the essence of our humanity with a divine reality determines the way in which we want to become instruments of a healing power much greater than our psychic powers. By aiming to meet another human being in our true wholeness and in theirs — that is essence and true Self-centredness — we can touch and activate the

45

healing power contained in a deeper reality of life. We are thus related to a cosmic order which "contains" so to speak, the universal criteria for true-self-relatedness to ourselves, to "the other"—indeed to the whole creation. This cosmic universal order may be designated as Truth manifesting itself in the Word. Not only the world's religions, but also mythology and science are partial expressions of this order—giving us conditioned insights into its timeless message. Unconditional insight comes to us as the Holy Spirit, the Spirit of Truth illumines our awareness and gives us a glimpse of the Source—the unconditioned deeper reality of life.

VII.

When we have a living relationship to the universal cosmic order and are open to the truth and vitality contained in the Source of Life—then we are free to relate spontaneously to life. Spontaneity thus understood is an important aspect of health. It is the up-welling of a deeper truth into the concrete reality of human relationships. Spontaneity must be clearly differentiated from impulsiveness. The latter is an expression of a momentary emotion; it may even be an expression of unrelatedness to a deeper reality of life. As an impulse it has a short or even instantaneous time dimension whereas spontaneity is a manifestation of a timeless reality. Emerging like a spring from the ground into sunlight, spontaneity is a response which cuts through the specific modes and rules of a given culture and/or the peculiarities of a given stage of development. If we are spontaneously related to the universal cosmic order and to the Source of Life we are centred in a way which enables us to grow and develop and thus to participate in the process of creation in terms of our unique potentialities.

Such an understanding of health necessitates a quality of relationship between the person who is an instrument of healing and the person to be healed quite different from what is called transference and counter-transference in psychoanalytical literature as we will show in Chapter 4. It is undoubtedly important to be aware of the nature of the transference/counter-transference relationship. But healing requires a meeting of the true self of two people, a meeting of their essence, a meeting as whole people. Only as the true self of the wounded person is unconditionally affirmed and the person is truly known can healing take place. The establishment of such a relationship is important in all three stages of the healing process.

The first stage is a systematic assessment of what I would call the "existential" situation of a person. By this I mean, first of all, an understanding of the "destiny" of a person. Who is this person truly meant to be and to become? What tasks are ahead of her or him? What is the fulfilment of this life or at least the next step on the way to fulfilment? Why does this person come *now* to be healed? These are the fundamental questions to be asked and to be related to the inner and outer resources available to the person in question. This requires a preliminary assessment of the nature and depth of the injury. The ways and methods used for this basic assessment may vary. Interviews in depth are likely to be most appropriate though any of the methods mentioned later may be useful.

In the second stage the healing process is systematically activated. The nature of this activation depends upon the person and the situation. The basic issue in this respect is the nature of the relationship between the Source of Life which contains the healing power of transformation and the source of injury which is constallated by the original wound, and which impedes or may even block the flow of the healing waters of life. In my experience the way in which the healing process may be stimulated and the time necessary for healing differ greatly depending upon the nature of this relationship and the strength of the source of healing in relation to the energies contained in the source of injury. People who were hurt with a similar intensity and whose wounds have a comparable depth may be healed in very different periods of time depending upon the extent and specific nature of the obstacles impeding the flow of the healing Source. The possible combinations are infinite, particularly if we take into consideration another important factor, namely, the ability of the power of the will to mobilize the energies of a deeper reality of life. The "outer" reality situation is also an important factor in this respect.

In a third stage the person to be healed takes a more and more active part — in understanding as well as in the ability to use the healing power alive in his or her own true self. When the second stage is initiated, the "healing" person must "carry" the wound of the person to be healed and must be the channel through which healing energy can flow. But as the healing process gains momentum, the healing power becomes more and more directly assessible to the person to be healed.

These three stages are not rigidly separated from each other. New insights about the nature of the injury may arise throughout the healing process and active participation on the part of the person to be healed may take place from the very beginning. However, these stages indicate a general pattern of significance for healing. Their understanding helps the way we guide this process and the combination of methods which we use.

IX.

The main methods which we use to implement such an understanding of health and healing are:
— meditation and contemplative prayer
— understanding of the language of the dreams and the ability to interpret them
— art and music as instruments of healing
— activation of the energy centres in the body and other ways of working through the body
— use of the healing energy in nature.

The extent of their use, the order and the combination of methods differ in each situation. Whenever possible meditation and contemplative prayer are central. The basic idea underlying the use of meditative practices and contemplative prayer is to facilitate as direct an approach to the Source of healing as possible. There are, however, situations in which an exploration of dreams is a precondition for opening up people to this Source. Even if this is not necessary, an approach interrelating meditation and understanding of dreams has proved most fruitful. Art and music can readily be interwoven with such an approach.

The activation of energy centres has a special significance as part of a true-self centred approach aiming to establish a living relationship to the personal and transpersonal source of life. Since each of the various energy centres is related to an aspect of the personality which has to be given attention in a holistic approach, true centredness implies a balance of the various energy centres in our bio-spiritual body. Though all the various centres are "recapitulated" in the head centre, our understanding of health and healing makes it imperative to give particular attention to the development of the heart centre. This centre balances our head and our lower parts in terms of our true feelings and values. Furthermore, if we imagine a person with outstretched arms (forming a cross), the vertical and the horizontal dimension of our body, symbolizing our relationship to the divine reality and to our fellow human beings, intersect at the heart. Our heart is the "seat" of our love and hence the centre of the integration of the individual-personal, the socio-economic and the transpersonal.

Though centred at the heart, our outreach to our fellow human beings — indeed to all life — must include our mind. Since holistic healing includes an understanding of human beings in their interrelationships and interactions with a wider human community and a deeper reality of life, we must be able to grasp the essential nature of the network of relationships forming the human community, the social order and the universal cosmic order. Depending upon the kind the persons we are, we may allow for a more intuitive or more intellectual understanding. This, however, is secondary to a living awareness of the universal ground of all life and of the way it manifests itself in a particular situation. Important in this connection is a relationship to the healing forces of nature. Our relationship to nature in general and to the earth in particular is of great importance for holistic healing.

X.

By integrating the various approaches and methods just outlined, growth and development of the whole person centred in the true self is truly fostered. A final question remains to be answered in this context: In which sense is our understanding of health and healing Christ- as well as true self-centred? It is Christ-centred inasmuch as Christ is a universal-cosmic reality alive in every human being,

and manifested in a fourfold way:
— as the Source of life
— as the power of transcendence enabling us to move
  towards true wholeness and oneness
— as ever renewing and ever forgiving
— as the logos of the universe.

Thus understood Christ is the essence of all that is and all that is in the process of becoming. In this universal cosmic sense Christ is the Source of life, the em-body-ment of the healing water of life. Christ also is—or denotes—the energy which makes possible a transformation from one state of being or consciousness to a higher state. Higher in this context means more differentiated and more integrated. The more differentiated a mode of consciousness, the more can the Spirit permeate our whole being. The more integrated, the more encompassing is our living relationship to others. Ultimately Christ is the transpersonal ground in which a true movement towards wholeness and oneness must be rooted. In this ground is an eternal spring making each day a new day because it is endowed with an ever renewing—and ever forgiving power. Being free from false guilt, free from resentment and hatred is an essential condition of health. Hence the capacity to be forgiven and to forgive is vital. Finally, Christ is also the logos of the universe expressing the true order of all life. As the logos Christ "gives us" the criteria to shape our own life as well as the social order in the light of the truth of the universal cosmic order. We are thus able to develop as healthy persons living an a healthy community.

Christ thus understood cannot be identified with the Judeo-Christian tradition but is alive in all human beings. The Word finds expression in many different words and ways of speaking. To make of Christ an exclusive reality is a sign of ill-health. The holistic health of the new era relates us creatively to all true life. Yet we deliberately remain within the Judeo-Christian tradition as a unique expression of the universal cosmic reality of Christ while being open to all religions, all world views — all human beings. In its deepest meaning health is expressed in a reverence for life and a relationship to people which defies words.

This is particularly true if we are concerned with an ultimate commitment to the mystery of life. Yet as human beings we must use words to communicate with each other. We therefore cannot avoid saying something about the mystery of the conjunction of the human and the divine. We may speak of Jesus of Nazareth (who is a historical figure) as the Christ, meaning He is endowed with the reality of the Christ power. I prefer this to the more usual Jesus Christ because the way the latter has often been used implies the danger of exclusiveness. But no matter how we express the mystery, Christ is not a word like any other word, it is not a name like another name. Christ is the Word denoting the essence of life. We must leave open the question as to other ways and manifestations of this power. Instead of feeling superior — a sign of ill-health — we follow the one who admonished us to make ourselves "last of all and servant of all". (Mark, 9, 35).

Fortunately we have now reached a stage in the evolutionary process which enables us to affirm the universality of Christ in a way which grounds us more deeply in the Judeo-Christian tradition while opening us up more freely to the whole creation. As we follow the One in whom the divine reality was so perfectly incarnated that he could heal instantaneously, we also know what it ultimately means to be centred in Christ: "Anything you did for one of my brothers here, however humble, you did for me." (Matthew 25, 40). This was said in a context reminiscent of (if not directly referring to) these words of Isaiah:

Is not this what I require of you as a fast:
to loose the fetters of injustice,
to untie the knots of the yoke,
to snap every yoke
and set free those who have been crushed?

Is it not sharing your food with the hungry,
taking the homeless poor into your house,
clothing the naked when you meet them
and never evading a duty to your kinsfolk?

Then shall your light break forth like the dawn
and soon you will grow healthy like a wound newly
healed. (Isaiah 58, 6—8)

Healing thus understood is conditional upon a caring attitude towards our fellow human beings while encompassing all aspects and spheres of life—from loosening "the fetters of injustice" to "clothing the naked" and doing our duty to those next to us. Isaiah relates healing to being able to "understand . . . know . . . see . . . listen" to the divine word. To "turn and be healed" is an aspect of such a relatedness to God.

Chapter 2

DEPTH PSYCHOLOGY AND SALVATION

I.

What is the relationship between healing as understood in the preceding chapter and salvation? We are exploring this question with special reference to the significance of depth psychology, that is, various approaches to an understanding of the deeper recesses of the human psyche and to developing ways of bringing them to conscious awareness. Examples are: psychoanalysis, analytical psychology, psychosynthesis, logotherapy, Gestalt therapy, etc. These as well as other approaches have made a major contribution to a new understanding of human nature and our ability to be instruments of healing: a contribution which is comparable to that made by natural science to a new understanding of nature in the post-medieval era. The basic question which we pose is: *What is the relationship between our personal development, our destiny on this earth and salvation?**

Salvation has many meanings. When I lived in the "Bible belt" of the United States, an evangelical minister came to me and begged me to say "I believe in Jesus Christ" because then I would be saved. In my own experience salvation is the fruit of a living relationship to that reality of life which is most alive in Christ, "the anointed one", the one in whom the holy flame burns in purity. It is true that Christ thus understood can not be limited to

---

* *For this chapter I have made considerable use of a paper given at a workshop of the Christian Student Community of the Free University of Berlin.*

Christianity. The Way, the Truth and Life which is manifested in Jesus of Nazareth expresses, as we have seen in the preceding chapter, a universal power of transformation and an ultimate knowledge of what is true and beautiful.

We may find this reality in a variety of ways and we may give different meanings to salvation. But the common denominator is a sense of liberation, of being released from the bondage of darkness, free to transcend pain, suffering and injustice — of being liberated from whatever separates us from our fellow human beings and from God. In its deepest meaning salvation denotes liberation from the contradictions of human experience, from all that denies the true divine order of Life and that interferes with the ultimate one-ness of all existence. Ultimately however salvation is not an individualistic matter, but touches our involvement in/with humankind. We share in suffering as long as one human being on this earth is suffering, as long as there is injustice in this world. This does not preclude a living awareness of a reality which transcends the contradictions of human experience and the darkness of our earthly existence. We may have a profound relationship of such a saving power whatever the circumstances of our life may be. Maximilian Kolbe, the priest in Auschwitz who voluntarily gave his life to save the life of a fellow prisoner, knew that transcending reality and its ultimate promise of salvation. He had the quality of relationship to life which gives the knowledge of salvation, a knowledge which is a reality *now* though it is a fore-knowledge inasmuch as it cannot be wholly "fulfilled" in this lifetime. The Kingdom of God is in us and is in this sense a present reality. But the fulfilment of the Kingdom has to wait until all humankind, the living and the dead, have "entered" it.

The relationship between depth psychology and salvation thus understood my be summed up in three propositions:

(1) Depth psychology can foster salvation by helping us to move from the "realm of the opposites" into "the realm of polarities". In doing so it helps us to be open to the Source of Life and to develop our true self.

(2) But it can only do this if it is not limited to an autonomous realm of the "psyche" but is, in its own understanding of human nature, recognizing a deeper reality of life manifesting itself in an "I-Thou" or trinitarian relationship.

(3) Yet ultimately salvation remains a reality far transcending depth psychology. It is therefore dangerous to confuse or identify the way of depth psychology and the way of salvation.

II.

The following story illustrates the first proposition.

A man told me that he felt completely empty, although he was a devout Christian who had always followed conscientiously and consistently the precepts of his religion, namely never to consider himself but to "lose" himself to live for others. To be faithful to this idea he spent all his free time with charitable and church activities. Yet he was far removed from the one who said: "I have come that men may have life, and may have it in all its fullness" (John 10, 10). Indeed he felt unfulfilled to the point of illness.

This man is an extreme illustration of a situation which I meet again and again in my therapeutic work: devout Christians, unfulfilled because they never dared to be truly themselves. They assumed that living for others meant "losing ourselves" without living our true self. Their "giving" was at the expense of their "receiving" what they needed for a full life and was not the kind of giving which "gave" to them while they were giving to others. Unable to "gain" their life "by losing it for (His) sake" (Matthew 10, 39) they could not give from the overflow of their heart thus enriching themselves while enriching others. Hence they could not experience St. Francis' knowledge that "it is in giving that we receive". At a deep level they experienced what they gave as a loss — thus living in the realm of the opposites of egoism and altruism without distinguishing between the true self and the little self. They were unable to live in the realm of the paradox expressed in the Biblical injunction: "Love your neighbour as yourself" (Matthew 22, 38). We must love ourselves by truly caring for the call to develop our God-given potentialities in order to become the kind of persons whom we are meant to be. This is the foundation for a self-giving love through which we receive more than we give rather than losing by giving.

We can best elucidate the fundamental difference between living in the realm of the opposites and in the realm of the paradox by having a brief look at the main stages of human development. They are:
— infancy and childhood
— development of our vocation, of our true unique self
— transcendence of "self", living as a "person in community"
— fulfilment.

These are not clearly separated stages of development. Yet there remains an important truth in looking at them as sequences in time because healthy growth is dependent upon our mastering the specific tasks inherent in each stage of development.

To be sound, a house must be built on firm foundations.

The same is true of our own development: the foundation built during our infancy and childhood is of greatest significance because we are then closest to cosmic forces which are much more powerful than our will-power. Hence we are most sensitive and vulnerable at a time when we are totally dependent upon others. The infant can literally do nothing for itself. It can only survive and develop through receiving the help and care of its parents — particularly its mother — shielding it from powerful forces. Indeed, the intensity of childhood experience can only be approximated by an adult who has preserved truly child-like qualities while being close to a deeper reality of life.

In infancy and childhood we are, furthermore, close to the opposites of human experience; light and darkness, joy and despair, love and hate are not yet part of a finely differentiated psychic structure but constitute energies which, though in separate realms, are so close to each other that an infant and child may move quickly from one extreme to the other. A child may be in tears at one moment and laugh the next moment — and truly experience both. A third factor is an infant and child's closeness to God, the ground of our being and the Source of life. The spontaneity of children testifies to this closeness. The infant and child gives a great deal of joy simply through its being close to a deeper reality of life and thus conveying the beauty of life.

Children live more in the world of fairy tales and fantasy than in the world of logic and sense-perceptions. This is particularly important since a child, not to speak of an infant, cannot differentiate between the images activated by the actual parents and those activated by deeper psychospiritual energies. These images interact or may even fuse. Willingly or not, all parents are therefore representatives of the divine as far as their children are concerned, no matter whether the parents consider themselves to be religious, agnostic or atheists. Hence they have a decisive influence on our openness to the Source of life.

The foundation of our ability to trust, to give and take and to have a sense of worth is laid in infancy and childhood. It is therefore essential that we receive what we need to meet the challenges which this stage presents. We must be surrounded by a "temenos", a holy circle formed by true love. To be true, love must express respect (and hence an inner distance rather than a "devouring" attitude), an unconditional affirmation based on the knowledge of who we essentially are (rather than making affirmation dependent upon what we do—whether or not we live up to the expectations of others) and an empathy rooted in an intuitive understanding of life (rather than a sentimentality covering up undeveloped parental emotions).

In the second stage, beginning with adolescence, the young person must complete the separation from parents and their world—which starts with birth—in order to find his or her own personally unique values and be able to discover his/her vocation and true self-hood. On the whole, this stage is intermediary inasmuch as giving and receiving is concerned. Receiving in an active sense remains primary while giving takes on new forms. The main contribution of this stage to healthy growth and development and to the knowledge of salvation is the formation of a strong centre which can withstand the pressures of collective forces, be they of a societal, cultural or of an archetypal psychological nature (these two expressions of collective forces are actually interrelated). At the same time the centre, to become the core of a healthy personality, must express those attitudes and values which constitute the unique true self of a person.

The third stage of transcendence of "self", of living as persons in community, is characterized by our receiving through giving. We have now reached a stage of development when we have established our true personally unique self and hence our primary orientation to life is one of giving. To be true, such giving must come from the over-flow of our heart — from the fullness of our being rather than as a result of a false altruism.

After decades, if not centuries of such false altruism being preached as a Christian virtue but in fact arising from an inability to distinguish between false ego-centredness and true-self centredness in Christ, it is important to emphasize the significance of healthy development through-out the first and second stages in order to be free to enter the third stage where we receive through giving. To be able to do so presupposes that we were free to receive and make our own the common human heritage in a way which enables us to become the kind of unique persons we essentially are. Uniqueness thus understood does not separate us from others. On the contrary, it makes us interrelated and interdependent, able to give and to take. Since our uniqueness consists in the unique combination of universal human qualities, the more truly we are aware of our own uniqueness, the more we are also aware of the uniqueness of others and of the need we mutually have of each other.

Provided we were given unconditional affirmation during the first stage and had the freedom of becoming true-self centred in the second stage, we are prepared not only to enter the third stage as healthy people but we also have the necessary foundation for a true fulfilment, of a progressive realization of our ability to receive through giving. To begin with, this ability may be expressed through the satisfaction of being able to give to other people what they need. As this process deepens we become free to find ourselves by losing ourselves for the sake of a deeper reality and truth. "Whoever cares for his own safety is lost; but if a man will let himself be lost for my sake, he will find his true self." (Matthew 16, 25). This is the highest or deepest relationship to ourselves and to others which we can achieve. When we have grown to that realization we have left the realm of opposites and entered the realm of paradox where we affirm our true self by losing somthing relatively less valuable and gaining something of much greater value.

Such a development is accompanied by deep changes in the whole "structure" of our personality manifesting themselves in a shift of the centre which enables us to let ourselves be "lost" and thus "gain" our true self as the centre of our being. This shift also enables us to live "as persons in community", as unique people aware of our common humanity. The deepest expression of such a mode of consciousness is a living awareness of being members of humanity united in oneness, members of the body of Christ. Such an awareness is a fruit of being on the Way—on our way and on that Way which transcends our mortal limitations and which was shown to us by the one who could say: "I am the Way, I am the Truth and I am Life" (John, 14, 6). To be on this Way will eventually. lead to the final "stage", a fulfilment that prefigures salvation. In the words of the Psalm: "to him who follows my way I will show the salvation of God" (Psalm 50, 23). Such an experience is the ultimate meaning of healthy growth and development understood as a road to salvation.

III.

When the path to health and salvation is blocked, because we did not receive the love needed to grow freely, we are wounded, we suffer and are unable to give truly. The way and the extent to which this is the case depends upon many factors. An extreme example of such a blockage, due to deprivation of true love by both parents is that of Kate, a deeply spiritual young woman who had a clear calling but was unable to actualize it. At a certain stage of transformation, when she had to meet the injuries of her infancy and childhood in order to become free, she brought a drawing of a man holding up a sword with a pierced heart. She wrote at the bottom of this drawing:

A bare, white stage, stark and hollow. A joker (the man) characterized and parodied as in a Walton Ashton ballet—macabre, sinister, carrying aloft and with great glee a human heart at the end of a sword. The odd and horrible thing is that tonight, as I try to think of it, part of me wants to jerk into the same rhythm and dance the same dance, as if participating in the glee."

Here is a picture of an injury and pain too great to be met creatively. When this happens we must react aggressively and destructively—unless we are shattered and become psychotic. Kate coped by identifying with the evil done to her: she was tempted to share "in the glee". Whether inner or outer-directed, such a response is typical of extreme situations. The police in concentration camps were often recruited among inmates identifying with their persecutors. The power of transcending the persecution— the pierced heart—is not within the grasp of the infant and child since the power of the divine and of the parent are fused. The actual father thus becomes the punishing

God-father and the relationship to God becomes precarious — as it did indeed for Kate.

During the session in which she brought the drawing of the pierced heart her body felt

> as if I was strangled. I can feel it all over my body. I can feel the sword — in my throat, my chest, my stomach . . . The worst thing was when the joker pierced my heart . . . I was just left in an empty space, there was nobody around, nobody who heard me cry, nobody to be with me, nobody in the whole world.

She now understood "why being alone is so unbearable that I fall asleep when my husband leaves the house" and why she felt "unlovable".

The need for warmth and understanding when we encounter as adults such a hitherto repressed infantile experience is well expressed in her "feeling like a bird who needs to be under its mother's wings". My room became "the only safe place" and intermittent phone calls had to ensure that I am here and understanding: "I am numb, I have no feeling, only a sense of unreality". Here is an echo of the inner emptiness and of the father-aggressor who made his daughter "a plaything" while the mother was standing piously in the background.

The day she experienced the pierced heart she saw on the street a child "looking eager, full of zest for life, about a year old". This encounter — as she said in the next session — made her feel "like dough being twisted by a screw. I felt my integrity being twisted, the joker's screw was cold, sharp, the dough was pushed through a hole." She had met the child she was meant to be and in the face of this reality she could see her present state clearly and experience the violence done to her integrity.

This shows how a deeply spiritual person was cut off from a living relationship to God and from the spontaneity and creativity of the Source of life. Though in a fundamentally good marriage with a most considerate husband, she was neither able to "give herself fully" nor to "take" the transforming potential of the warmth and love which was offered to her though without these she could not have survived. Nor was she free to follow her true calling. She could not, therefore, move adequately from infancy-childhood into the second stage of growth, the development of her vocation and of her true unique self. She was not free to give up her child-ish qualities while preserving her child-like ones. The firm ground on which to build her life, to follow her vocation and to develop her unique self was missing. She was free neither from parental nor from societal authorities.

These two kinds of authority are related but not identical. We may be free from the personal authority of the parents yet remain caught in societal-cultural attitudes and ideas which are incompatible with our true unique self-development because they express values different from those constituting our own true self. A classical example of a combination of these two kinds of authorities is the dream Frances Wickes records in her book *The Inner World of Choice*:

I am driving a hand car through a long tunnel. The roof is so low that I have to crouch in a way that cramps every muscle. I feel that I will smother if I do not soon come out into the open; but the tunnel goes on and on, stretching endlessly into the same dreary darkness. As I wake, gasping for breath, I see the hand car. On each side is painted, 'B&O RR'.

64

The "Baltimore & Ohio" was the family railroad on which the family "travelled with passes of inherited prestige. The family fortune, traditions, conventions, were indissolubly linked to this road. No member of the family had ever thought of running off these tracks any more than would one of the cars start off into the open on its own initiative."[1]

Another example of the quest for true selfhood from my own work is the dream of a young man who lived in a kind of veneration of his superior and of the values he stood for until he dreamt that this man "is all mouth" — no real substance, no true values. Another example is of a woman who had not dared to follow her artistic vocation. She dreamt: "Somebody comes to me and says I should paint. My daughter is also there. I have short hair but I should have long hair. I am in a dressing room, there is a niche with holy water. I use it . . ." This dream had an "annunciation quality"; an inner reality has been awakened ("Somebody comes to me") which admonishes her to actualize her God-given talent. She described her daughter as struggling to find her own way, symbolizing the new life in herself. The hair symbolizes the strength — as it did for Samson, and the dressing room the new garment that she is about to wear — a garment which expresses her true self. The holy water is the living water which Jesus gave to the woman at the well, "an inner spring welling up for eternal life" (John 4, 14).

For another woman the awakening of her own true self was announced in this dream: "I am in a small dark room, I hear a man's voice, shouting. There is another man on a stretcher, stitched down . . . like Lazarus." The male voice shouting was the still imprisoned voice of her own masculinity which was about to be freed. Unlived, dead until now, like Lazarus, the voice was brought back to

65

life, calling her to recognize her own strength and potentialities.

A final illustration is from a person with a deep spirituality and creativity: "There are many people around . . . like dots; I go to them for affirmation. In the middle is something different. A voice says: 'go to the centre'." As long as we need affirmation from the many people around — the dots — we remain limited if not imprisoned by parental and/or societal ideas and values. To become the kind of people we are meant to be we must follow the often "still small voice" which says "go to the centre". There we find our true unique self as well as a reality transcending it.

These examples must suffice to show that certain conditions in our personal development must be fulfilled to enable us to follow our God-given vocation. We must have a solid foundation for the development of our true self and must have the inner strength to be masters in our own house. These qualities, in turn, presuppose that we must have freely received the love and understanding essential to master the challenge of infancy and childhood. We must have become firm in our selfhood in order to free ourselves from parental and societal authority and to follow the voice of true authority. This voice calls us to actualize our vocation by becoming centred in our true self.

IV.

Depth psychology can help us a great deal to find our way. It has an important contribution to make to the unfolding of our true self. Crucial in this connection is its ability to remove obstacles and blocks which separate us from the

Source of life which nourishes our true self. Though the reasons why people may be cut off from this source are manifold, the common root is lack of the kind of affirmation which is necessary for an infant and child to feel secure and hence free to express him- or herself. The result of such a deprivation is activation of the opposites manifesting itself in hatred and aggression (directed against ourselves or others) as well as anxiety and guilt. The forces in this process are so powerful that the infant and child must build walls if not castles for protection. It must entrench itself in order to be sure that nobody can violate its core, its inner sanctum, and thus destroy the essence of its personhood. Ultimately neurosis is an attempt to safeguard the essential true self from dangerous invasion. The forces mustered for protection—like the forces which are attacking—have cosmic power. Hence the fortresses which were originally meant for protection often become seemingly impenetrable prison walls.

To break open these walls requires time and patience. Like the conquest of Jericho, the walls must be circumvented again and again until they can fall and creative energies can bring about a transformation. This process is often expressed in the birth—or appearance—of a child which symbolizes new life. A person who felt paralysed before she began to struggle with the forces imprisoning her experienced release when she dreamed about a newly born baby. Her dream conveyed a sense of precariousness and fear that there might not be enough love for the baby as well as an awareness of deep suffering. This was a reflection of her own baby-hood while at the same time indicating a re-birth.

Another woman in whom new life began to stir had the following dream: "I am in a room . . . there is the Christ child . . . but it needs protection from the world . . . There is a screen around it." This dream indicates a first awareness of liberation. The new life still needs protection from the world. The dreamer could not yet face the world and be a creative transforming influence in it. A good deal of growth had to take place before this was possible. Yet the promise of the Christ-child is already alive.

As the blocks which are in the way to the Source of life are removed, new vistas open. Crossing a river may symbolize this process of transformation as it does in the following dream: "I am on the banks of a river. The river is wide. I can scarcely see the other side. I feel I must build a bridge across it. I think of building a number of pillars to have a safe passage. But a voice says: you must build the bridge with one span across the river." This dream indicated an inner readiness and need to make a jump — to dare to go into a future scarcely visible yet already known at a deeper level.

The examples given illustrate the manner in which depth psychology can help us to find our way. It is true that these illustrations refer to situations where blockages had to be removed in order to open the way to the Source of life. But the significance of depth psychology is not limited to such situations. It has a contribution to make whenever we move towards new insights and struggle to realize our — ever growing — awareness of truth and beauty whenever and wherever growth and development are desired and fostered.

Human beings do not grow like trees, simply unfolding the potential contained in the seed. We grow by overcoming conflicts, by heightening our awareness, by struggling to overcome the opposites and to move into the realm of the paradox. "Discernment" is essential to know the often fine lines which separate what is true and what is false. The struggle to keep the water of life from being polluted and to find the truth in ever more articulate, more "refined" ways is a universal struggle of all human beings at all times.

In the Bible this struggle is first experienced as a struggle against the "idols made by human hands". "Knowledge (and) discernment" were considered essential "to walk in the light of the Lord" (Isaiah 1, 3 and 5). Whenever people strayed from the path of truth, they felt they had aroused God's anger, which they experienced as an act "to refine away (our) base metal . . . and purge all (our) impurities" (Isaiah 1, 25) in order to give the knowledge and discernment necessary to be "healed". This expresses well a process of "refinement", of differentiation for which depth psychology has found effective ways. But the basic struggle to find the true God goes on throughout human history and is likely to continue till the end of time. It is a universal struggle which begins as soon as we become conscious of the human condition. All of us are somehow caught in the underground den described by Plato where the truth we apprehend is "literally nothing but the shadows of the images" (*The Republic,* Book VII). All of us see at times, as St. Paul put it, "only puzzling reflections in a mirror." (1 Cor. 13, 12). Yet we are now able to acquire a knowledge and learn a discernment not open to previous generations. The insights and methods developed by depth psychology can help us in a new way to be open to the Source and to keep the water of life pure.

V.

I am fully aware of the implications of such a claim for the significance of depth psychology. I must, therefore, introduce an important qualification formulated in my second proposition, namely that depth psychology must not be limited to an autonomous realm of the psyche but must recognize a deeper reality of life. This applies to the depth-psychological understanding of human nature as well as to the practice of the therapist who must be in an open relationship to the Source of life.

Whenever we meet another human being in depth, a third dimension is activated which transcends the two people seen as two separate individuals. The nature of this third element may vary within a range defined by two poles: by a projection of unconscious aspects of our psyche on the other person and by a "resonance" of a shared deeper reality of life.

To project as already mentioned means to "put" something "on" or "into" another person which is actually primarily in us. The other may evoke a response which has more to do with our own inner situation than with the reality of the other person. We may project on a man whom we meet the image formed by our experience of our father, brother or previous boyfriend. We may "see" in others negative—or positive—tendencies which are actually alive in us. Briefly, "the other" may become a screen on which we project a picture alive in us. However, unlike a mechanical projection, the screen on which we project is never completely blank. Another person is likely to evoke a projection by virtue of having some—maybe quite incidental—similarity with the projected image. Furthermore, a projection has its roots in a deeper, transpersonal reality and hence has a transpersonal power. It activates a reality which transcends two individuals and which constitutes the "third dimension" in their relationship. It may, therefore, have an uplifting or even a demonic quality.

Quite different is the possibility of a creative relationship to a transpersonal reality. When two people meet in their essence, at the core of their being, they are touching a truly shared deeper reality of life. They enter a relationship nourished by the Source of Life. They can see each other truly and their perception is illumined by a transpersonal light. We may "fall in love" with another person and find out laster that we do not really love the person as he or she actually and essentially is. The "loved" person may have aroused certain projections in us which vanished as time went on. But if we truly love another person, a deeper reality sanctifying our love comes alive.

In an actual human relationship both poles are likely to be activated: a deeper reality is coming to life but we also project something on the other person. This is also true in the relationship of the therapist and the person seeking to be healed. In the psycho-analytical literature the problem of projections has hitherto been prominent. There is no doubt that the greatest possible consciousness of this mechanism is essential in order to avoid interference with the healing process. But the healing power alive in this process is not mediated through what has been called "the transference/counter-transference" relationship — briefly mentioned in Chapter 1 — which is essentially a projective mechanism, rather it comes alive through a quality of relatedness in which a shared deeper reality of life which unites us at our centre, in our essence, is activated. A pre-condition for this to happen is that the therapist must have a living relationship to this reality.

When two people meet in their true essence, the truth of Christ comes alive. "For where two or three have met together in my name, I am there among them." (Matthew 18, 20). In Martin Buber's language an "I-Thou" as distinguished from "I-it" relationship has been established. The latter is the kind of relationship in which people are objects—or objects of projection. The former is "the cradle of the Real Life,"[1] the foundation of every true human relationship and community:

> *The true community does not arise through peoples having feelings for one another (though indeed not without it), but through, first, their taking their stand in living mutual relation with a living Centre, and, second, their being in living mutual relations with one another. The second has its source in the first, but is not given when the first alone is given. Living mutual relation includes feelings, but does not originate with them. The community is built up out of living mutual relation, but the builder is the living effective Centre.*[3]

The "I-Thou" relationship thus understood is the key and precondition for depth psychology making a meaningful contribution to salvation. Only by establishing a relationship between the therapist and person seeking healing which is rooted in and nourished by "the living, effective Centre" can the healing, transforming energy of that deeper reality which is also alive in salvation become effective. To say this does not identify healing with salvation. But it makes healing an aspect of salvation rather than a cure of symptoms. It makes the kind of healing which depth psychology has to offer an expression of that living Centre—our true self—where the cosmic Christ, alive in every human being, manifests itself. Christ thus understood is the bread of Life which nourishes; the water of life which purifies; the light of consciousness which gives us "knowledge and discernment"; and finally the truth which makes us free.

The cosmic Christ alive in an "I-Thou" relationship can not be limited to any one religion or group. The transforming reality of Christ is alive in all of us. It manifests itself in infinite ways—depth psychology being one of them. At a time in history when the spirit was often congealed in traditional forms which had lost their meaning, the discoveries of depth psychology made a uniquely significant contribution. This is the reason why Paul Tillich could say: "In depth psychology there is frequently more awareness of the meaning of grace and, consequently, more effective 'care of souls' than in the ministry of the church."[4] The grace "bestowed" through depth psychology is the grace of finding one's true self and/or being able to realize it more fully. It is the grace of an open relationship to the living Centre of the universe. By saying that this grace is "bestowed" through depth psychology we have summed up its deepest meaning—and its dependency on a reality transcending it. For grace signifies something freely given, bestowed on us as a gift, not something we can account for as resulting from a specific action of ours—granted that it is not unrelated to an inner attitude of "doing the truth".

VI.

Such an understanding of grace brings us to our third proposition, namely, that although depth psychology can make a meaningful contribution to salvation, it is dangerous to confuse or identify the two. Ultimately salvation touches a reality far beyond anything a human being can do or not do. In its deepest meaning it is a mystery veiled from the limitations of human perception and understanding.

73

As human beings we are saved through knowledge of the divine reality: "You shall know the truth, and the truth will set you free" (John 8, 32); "This is eternal life, to know thee who alone art truly God, and Jesus Christ whom thou hast sent" (John 17, 3). Knowing in this context means more than the meaning we often give to this word in everyday language. If I say "I know John" I may simply mean that I met him, spoke to him or saw him on various occasions. But it does not mean that I really know what kind of a person he is. The Hebrew word which is translated as "know" in the Old Testament has a very different meaning. It expresses the depth and intimacy of a relationship. To know someone at depth presupposes a quality of relationship which enables us to penetrate to the centre of a person. Unless I can "see" the true self of another person with my inner eye, I do not truly know that person. Analogously, to be saved through "knowing" means a quality of relationship which enables me to "see" the divine reality. I must have experienced the essence of this reality to know it in a way which makes me free and allows me to consciously participate in eternal life.

Salvation thus understood has a twofold meaning: I "am" saved through knowing God but "being" saved is not a static achievement, not an accomplished fact but a way of "becoming". This is the reason why Jesus said: "I am the Way" and not "I am the Goal". Yet the "I am" also expresses the reality of "being". In a deep sense of entering into the mystery of the union of the human and the divine, Jesus as the Christ is also the goal but a goal which can not be reached on this earth. Our life on earth is a pilgrimage; though centred in a timeless reality we are, except for moments of ecstacy, "on the way"—unless we are in a side alley, or on a road without issue.

To "be on the way" means an awareness of a reality transcending the manifest injustices of life, the pain and suffering around us—all the contradictions of human experience. To know such a reality is the common foundation of all salvation. However, there are many forms which the quest for salvation may take. Three basic expressions are: (1) a withdrawal from the world; (2) an intermingling of the divine reality perceived as bringing salvation with some aspects of this world; and (3) a dynamic interrelation and interaction between our knowledge of the divine reality and an involvement with this world.

Once having experienced a reality of light, love and harmony, a peace "which is beyond our utmost understanding" (Phil, 4, 7), there is a natural urge to stay in it. There may also be a need to withdraw from the world in order to gain the inner strength to live the newly-found reality. Such a withdrawal may take many forms. It may be temporary or it may be in the permanent commitment of a religious vocation as hermit or monk. It is not accidental that devout Christians preferred to live as hermits when Christianity became a Roman state religion. Yet the monastic life, though it means a withdrawal from the world does not necessarily mean an abandonment of a transforming influence on it as many medieval monastic orders have shown. The first Protestant monastic community since the Reformation, Taizé, has a deeply transforming influence in this world.

The divine reality may also be identified with a temporal socio-political institution. Theocracy is a classical example. The medieval world had a strong theocratic element (though it was in no way a true theocracy), and the Puritans in New England attempted to build the holy city on this earth. Today we recognize the danger of identifying time and eternity by giving a divine sanction to temporal institutions. We are struggling to move on to a new mode of awareness in which the divine becomes a dynamic power of transformation.

The third form expresses this quest to "use" a living experience of a transcending reality as a power for transforming this world. God and the world are not identified but stand in a creative tension with God acting on and in this world through us. Having "been" saved through a living relationship to the divine reality, we are enabled to participate in "building" the kingdom. Being and Becoming are interrelated in such an experience. Salvation has happened and is happening at the same time. We partake of the paradox of "knowing" eternal life while being in this temporal body on this earth. Since the kingdom of God is "within" as well as "without", immanent as well as transcendent, we can know this kingdom now while living in this world. This creative tension thus aroused has a twofold meaning of transformation and transcendence. Inasmuch as we know the Kingdom, we have transcended the contradictions of daily exprience, and "eternal life" is a present reality. Inasmuch as we also recognize our human condition, of being 'always on the way' we attempt to transform "what is" into "what ought to be".

This form of salvation—of "being in the world but not of the world"—presupposes a movement from the realm of opposites into the realm of polarities or paradox. It unites receptivity towards the divine reality with a transforming thrust in this world. It also unites peacefulness and struggle. We partake of the peace of Jesus "such as the world cannot give" (John 14, 27) while struggling to realize this peace in our daily lives and in the human community of which we are part.

The height and depth of such an experience of life is

our participation in the life, death and resurrection of Jesus of Nazareth. In his life, he manifested the quality of a living relationship to God which bestows the power of transformation, the power to heal which is also the power to free from sin. In his death he manifested the deepest relatedness to his fellow human beings which a human being can achieve by suffering *for* others rather than turning against them. This brought him closer to *their* true selves than they were themselves. Only a human being wo is in a profound relationship to humankind can say while bleeding on the cross: "Father forgive them; they do not know what they are doing." (Luke 23, 34). In saying this Jesus affirmed their—and our—true selves. In this sense he "saved us", cleansed us of our sins, through giving his blood. He thus showed us the way and the ultimate meaning of salvation.

We are "on the way" as we follow him in sharing the suffering of this world in the same spirit as he did. Such an inner participation enables us to partake of the resurrection which manifests a reality and power transcending all the contradictions of human experience—even death. This power can come alive in us too as we discover in us the potential of the same quality of relatedness to life. In Jesus "the son of man", this potential is alive in its essence and purity. In Jesus "the son of God" this potential has become actuality. The spirit of God in whose image we have been created unites this twofold sonship. All of us are called to actualize our God-given potential: "For all who are moved by the Spirit of God are sons of God". (Romans 8, 14).

Depth psychology can help us to respond to this call by realizing our humanity so fully that we are led by the divine spirit. It can also help us to develop a living faith manifesting itself in commitment and action. To "believe"

77

in Jesus means salvation if our belief is a living reality. Such belief or faith is participation, partaking, words which combine "taking" with "active involvement". This combination has an element of mystery — as has the destiny of each of us. We may call it the mystery of the union of opposites — that is their transcendence in polarities. But in doing so we have only renamed the mystery. Equally great is the mystery of being able to participate so fully in the life, death and resurrection of a human being who lived 2000 years ago, that He becomes alive in us.

By partaking *now* of the life, death and resurrection of Jesus of Nazareth, who in eternity is the Christ, we unite "being" and "becoming". We are saved though we are aware of not yet being saved. This "not yet" indicates the limitations of salvation in a world of injustice, pain and suffering. It also indicates our knowledge that if we are truly involved with humankind we cannot be saved as long as there is injustice and suffering anywhere in this world. Nor can we be "saved" without knowing that those who lived before us have been or will be saved — that the injustice done to them and their suffering will be or has been redeemed. In saying this I am going beyond human comprehension, beyond anything a human being can 'do'. I may say I "know" the power of God to be able to accomplish this. But I cannot say more. I may intuit the form and manifestation of that power. Yet ultimately I can only acknowledge a mystery and I must be content to say with St. Paul:

O depth of wealth, wisdom, and knowledge of God! How unsearchable his judgments, how untraceable his ways! Who knows the ways of the Lord? . . . Source, Guide, and Goal of all that is — to him be glory for ever! Amen. (Romans 11, 33–36)

Notes

1. Frances Wickes, *The Inner World of Choice,* Coventure Ltd., London, 1977, p.3.

2. Martin Buber, *I and Thou,* T. & T. Clark, Edinburgh, 1950, p.9.

3. *Ibid.,* p. 45

4. Paul Tillich, *The Protestant Era,* University of Chicago Press, 1948, p.134.

Chapter 3

THE HEALING CHURCH

I.

The theme of The Healing Church* is closely linked to the issues with which we were concerned in the previous chapter. Indeed in the Bible healing is ultimately understood as an expression of a divine power. It is a cosmic event: "The moon shall shine with a brightness like the sun's, and the sun with seven times its wonted brightness, seven days light in one when the Lord binds up the broken limbs of his people and heals their wounds." (Isaiah 30, 26).

The meaning of the Healing Church is most articulately expressed in Isaiah's prophecies about Jesus' self-sacrifice:

> *Behold, my servant shall prosper,*
> *he shall be lifted up, exalted to the heights*
> . . . . .
> *Yet on himself be bore our sufferings,*
> *our torments he endures*
> . . . . .
> *Yet the Lord took thought for his tortured servant*
> *and healed him who has made himself a sacrifice for*
> *sin* (Isaiah 52, 13; 53, 10).

We touch here the deepest meaning of healing as a relationship to God enabling us to affirm our fellow human beings unconditionally and thus helping them to become free

* *This Chapter is based on a talk given at All Saints Church in Fleet in 1979.*

while freeing us to bear their wounds. These are indeed essential ingredients of true healing. In Jesus they were present in their ultimate power: through renunciation he became a pure channel of the divine power to heal.

There are many examples in the Gospel of healing the sick, driving out evil spirits, making the blind see, making the deaf hear, making the lame walk and ultimately of bringing the dead back to life. It is significant that Jesus' first act after having delivered the Sermon on the Mount was to heal the leper. For him healing and entering the Kingdom of God were closely related.

Yet the Biblical concept of healing has a wider significance than that which we usually understand by this word today. The words to be able to "see", to be "opened", to be able to walk, correspond to Jesus' repeated call "to see", "to hear" and "to act" in such a way that we partake of the Kingdom of God: "He now called the twelve together and gave them power and authority to overcome all the devils and to cure diseases, and sent them to proclaim the Kingdom of God and to heal." (Luke 9, 1—2). This is not merely a juxta position of words but indicates an inner connection. When Jesus had "driven out a devil which was dumb" (Luke 11, 14), an argument arose how he did it. Some said that he had done it by the power of Beelezebub. In repudiating this charge, he said: "If it is by the finger of God that I drive out devils, then be sure the Kingdom of God has already come upon you." (Luke 11, 20).

The very language which Jesus spoke, Hebrew, does not separate the spiritual, the psychological and the social-communal, as is still typical of today's world view. When he said 'shalom', he meant peace in the deepest sense of balance, harmony and true relatedness to life. Jesus, like the Old Testament prophets, was concerned with the whole person, healing was "holistic", it had a transpersonal meaning with reference to the human community and to God.

Healing thus understood is never a one-way act. It takes place in relationship as we have seen in the preceding chapter. The quality of relatedness necessary for the Church to be a healing Church is the kind of faith alive in Abraham, Jesus and St. Paul—trust and openness to the divine reality. Jesus said to the woman whom he healed of her haemorrhages: "Your faith has healed you." (Matth. 9, 22). When he received a message from the President of the Synagogue that it was too late to come because his daughter was already dead, Jesus said "Do not be afraid, only have faith"—and he healed his daughter. (Mark 5, 36). In his own home town Jesus was unable to heal because people had no faith in him. (Matth. 13, 58).

Healing as understood in the Bible, is an expression of the power of transformation encompassing all spheres of life. It touches the depth and height of human experience. This may be why Jesus called his disciples "fishers of men". A fish is a symbol of the deep contents of what is often called "the unconscious" and what I would rather call a deeper reality of life. The fish was also a symbol used by the early Christians. It is a universal symbol of transformation, of life at a deep level. In this sense it is a symbol of partaking of the Body of Christ.

II.

The Body of Christ is "the carrier" as well as the "proto-type" or "image" of the healing ministry of the church:

The carrier, because it "contains" the power of transformation and of healing, and the prototype or image, because the Body of Christ indicates the nature and the meaning of health.

Paul experienced the Body of Christ as having three essential characteristics: it is universal and cosmic; in it each member follows his or her calling or vocation; and finally, all members stand in a relationship of mutuality, caring for each other because ultimately they are one. These three aspects are interrelated: being one signifies a total harmony of true self-realization and true self-giving. The former requires that we follow our God-given vocation, the latter that we are free to give its fruit in a living relationship to humankind, indeed to the whole creation. Such freedom presupposes openness to the universal ground and Source of all life.

Paul expressed this interrelationship in his image of Christ "like a single body with its many limbs and organs, which, many as they are, together make up one body." (10 Cor. 12, 12). The one-ness of the Body of Christ is highlighted by the reference to Jews and Greeks—the opposite world views of antiquity—as being part of this Body. The Greek world view was rational and sense-related, the Hebrew mystic and intuitive. In the language of our time "Western" and "Eastern" world views could be substituted for "Greek" and "Jew". This illustrates Paul's understanding of the universality of the Body of Christ. In its deepest meaning the Body of Christ is the body of humankind united in one-ness. All of us belong essentially and potentially to this body, and all those grasped by the Spirit of Truth are members of this body.

Paul describes vividly and beautifully the unity of our body as an analogy to the Body of Christ:

*A body is not a single organ, but many . . . Suppose the
foot should say, 'Because I am not a hand I do not
belong to the body': it does belong to the body none
the less. Suppose the ear were to say, 'Because I am not
an eye, I do not belong to the body': it does still belong
to the body!*   (1 Cor. 12, 14—16).

Each member of the Body of Christ has his or her
unique function and vocation: "God appointed each limb
and organ to its own place in the body, as he chose."
(1 Cor. 12, 18). To be a member of the Body of Christ
means to be truly self centred and thus to be related to—
indeed be part of—the Centre of all life. It also means
to be in a relationship of mutuality to our fellow human
beings, caring for each other because we are ultimately
one.

*God has combined the various parts of the body, giving
special honour to the humbler parts, so that there might
be no sense of division in the body, but that all its
organs might feel the same concern for one another.
If one organ suffers, they all suffer together. If one
flourishes, they all rejoice together.* (1 Cor. 12, 24—26).

If we want to rejoice together, we must also be able to
suffer together: "Help one another to carry these heavy
loads, and in this way you will fulfil the law of Christ.
(Gal. 6, 2). A chassidic saying expresses this beautifully:
"If it so happens that you see a sin in somebody else or
hear about it, search for your share in it and strive to
improve yourself. Then the other will find a new way—
provided you encompass him in the spirit of unity because
all of us are one human being."[1]

Such a depth of understanding of the ultimate meaning
of life explains why we referred to the Body of Christ as

"the carrier" as well as "the prototype" of the healing ministry of the Church: Paul's understanding of the Body of Christ as universal, giving to each person a function corresponding to our true self and making us a mutually caring community describes clearly the meaning of health and healing. In this sense the Body of Christ is the proto-type, the image of health; it indicates the goal of healing. This Body also "contains" the healing power, the power to make us one, whole. In this sense the Body of Christ is "the carrier".

Jesus said repeatedly that power went out of him in the process of healing. (Mark 5, 30). He was equally emphatic in saying that God is the ultimate source of this power. "God is the source of my being and from him I come." "I am not myself the source of the words I speak to you; it is the father who dwells in me doing his own work." (John 14, 10). To be healthy, to be healed ultimately means to be nourished by the Source of life, which is the living expression of God's love for us. It means to be open to the transforming power contained in this Source, to drink "the living water" which is "an inner spring always welling up for eternal life".

As we do so, we partake of the body of Christ—and take part in the creation. We help to build a human community in which all human beings can be creative, by fulfilling the divine call to gain their true self. To be truly healthy is a dynamic process, not a static condition. It means infinitely more than absence of illness, cure of symptoms, or individual wellbeing in a suffering world. It means growth, development, active involvement in the evolu-tionary process. It encompasses the totality of our relation-ships to Life—all spheres of life, family, work, public life. It is a struggle with the powers of darkness, of ego-centricity. It touches all fibres of our being.

III.

In order to understand the healing ministry we must know the relationship between the Body of Christ, understood as the true Church, and the various churches. We must also know how all of us can, as members of the Body of Christ, partake individually and corporately in the healing ministry.

If we were wholly imbued by the spirit of Christ; if the various churches were wholly united with the Body of Christ, then the healing Church and the various churches would be identical. But this is not so. The churches are composed of full-blooded human beings and they are part of culturally and historically unique societies which are but partial expressions of a universal Truth. Ideas and world views change in the course of history. Our feelings, emotions and our experience of life also change as consciousness develops. Hence, no church can express the *whole* truth.

This is obvious when looking back in time or looking at other cultures and civilizations. Today we do not consider the burning of witches to be a holy act. Nor do we consider kings and emperors to have a divine sanction. Yet these views dominated the Western world for centuries. Looking at other cultures we can readily see that the "holy wars" proclaimed by Islam were not an expression of divine truth. Yet the same spirit permeated Christianity for hundreds of years. What was true then is in some way also true today. The human condition imposes itself on our outlook on life and on our knowledge of the Truth. In the words of Paul:

Are there prophets? Their work will be over.
Are there tongues of ecstacy? They will cease.
Is there knowledge? It will vanish away:

86

*for knowledge and prophecy alike are partial, and the
partial vanishes when wholeness comes . . .
Now we see only puzzling reflections in a mirror, but
then we shall see face to face.*   (1 Cor. 13, 8—10, 12).

Just as knowledge and prophecy are partial, limited by
the space-time in which we are, so our ability to encompass the totality of the relationships which constitute
health is limited. We are never "whole"; only at rare
moments are we truly "one". In the short span of our
lives we can realize only some of our potentialities. Hence
our share in the ministry of healing is also partial. Yet we
can be in a living, centred relationship to the Body of
Christ. We can be a unique organ in this Body truly related
to it provided we are true-self centred.

If this is the case and we actualize our true essence, we
experience a creative tension between our present partiality
and our search for wholeness. As members of a particular
church we may experience a creative tension in relation to
the universal-cosmic Body of Christ—the true Church—
with its ever renewing power of the Spirit of Truth. The
transforming power of Christ is alive in such a creative
tension wherever we may "be" at a particular moment in
time—as persons, as members of the human community,
or as members of our churches.

We can thus struggle ever more intently for justice and
for fellowship. As we do so "the kingdom of God has
already come upon (us)"; we are "like yeast, which a
woman took and mixed with half a hundredweight of
flour till it was all leavened." (Matth. 13, 33). As the
yeast transforms the flour to nourishing bread, so can we
develop a mode of consciousness enabling us to partake
of the healing, transforming power alive in the Body of
Christ. We can become agents of transforming "what is"

into "what ought to be". Though partial and limited we can partake of the oneness and wholeness which is ours in Christ and be transformed and renewed as we are helping others to be renewed and transformed.

As we do so we stand in a creative tension to the universal true Church. This presupposes a clear distinction between the various churches and the Church understood as the Body of Christ. It also implies a challenge for an ever growing ability to discern what is universally true and what is time-bound. The following prayer which Pope John XXXIII said shortly before he died is a deeply moving example of a new discernment as our consciousness becomes more wholly centred:

> *We recognize now that throughout many, many centuries, blindness has covered our eyes. Hence we can not see any more the beauty of thy chosen people and cannot recognize any more in their faces the features of our first born brother. We recognize that the sign of Cain is on our foreheads. For centuries Abel has been lying in blood and tears because we have forgotten thy love. Forgive us the curse which we unjustly spoke over the name of the Jews. Forgive us that we crucified Thee in their curse for a second time. For we did not know what we were doing.*"[2]

This prayer shows that the churches were not able to express the whole truth and were hence unable to fulfil a true healing ministry. It also opens doors for the churches to become a true Church of reconciliation transcending *all* divisions and healing all separations in order to be an ever truer expression of the Body of Christ.

IV.

How can we, you and I, serve ever more faithfully the True Church and thus creatively participate in the healing process? This query is part of a wider question concerning the relationship between our individual and our corporate witness and healing function.

While fully recognizing that "There are varieties of gifts . . . There are varieties of service . . . There are many forms of work . . ." (1 Cor. 12, 4—6), and that each of us is called in a personally unique way, what is primary is our corporate witness, our shared vision of a true human community grounded in our knowledge of Christ as the Logos of the universe. The Truth of Christ is an all encompassing truth relevant for all aspects and spheres of life. This is clearly expressed in Paul's understanding of the Body of Christ as the prototype of a true, that is healthy, human community in which every human being participates through development of his or her true self.

However, to be real, alive, something to act upon, such a vision must be spelled out in a way which makes it possible to relate it concretely to the existing order. An approach which I consider fruitful is the development of "middle axioms", that is of fundamental guidelines or principles which form a bridge between our vision and daily life. These principles have been called "middle axioms" because they are neither so general that they mean little or nothing concretely, nor so specific as to exclude differences in their practical application. They are in "the middle" between these two extremes without losing any of their fundamental nature or practical usefulness. Middle axioms are rooted in the Bible and express its universal truth yet they are applicable to the existing social institutions. An example already mentioned in

Chapter 1 is the proposition that a human being should always be an end and never be a means for the purposes of other people. Equally, money should never be an end but only a means. Inasmuch as our social institutions are means-end structures, these two guidelines can be quite concretely applied. They are the foundation of a social witness which constitutes a cutting edge in moving towards a true human community. At the same time these guidelines leave room for alternative answers and solutions of specific issues.

It is not too long ago that a well-known theologian said:—

> *Is it not a sign of terrifying helplessness that theology which has developed the most articulate approach to historical and systematic issues does not even have the most essential categories to comprehend the social reality of the life and work of countless human beings?*"[3]

This is a harsh judgment. Fortunately we have made some progress since these words were pronounced, but basically they still remain true today. The development of a meaningful social witness without which the churches cannot adequately fulfil their healing ministry remains an important task and serious challenge.

Beside needing a vision we need a bridge relating the vision to our daily life. The guiding principles forming this bridge are the Way which Jesus showed us, the Way of love alive in true-self relatedness. Love in Christ is not a sentimental attitude but a quality of relatedness rooted in a deep knowledge and understanding of others. This is the way of non-violence, the way of a non-violent struggle. It implies dialogue, respect for personal uniqueness and recognition that the answers to specific issues may be different. It also requires the ability to take suffering upon ourselves rather than inflict it on others.

While emphasizing again that each of us has been called to make our own personally unique contribution to the healing ministry and that there is room for genuine differences of opinion as to how best to implement the shared fundamental guidelines, the need for corporate action in our time is imperative. It can be fully actualized while truly respecting our personhood provided we follow an open experimental approach. There is indeed a vital need for small experiments, for new models, for an exploration of new ways of building true human communities.

The early Christians had a very clear model.

All whose faith had drawn them together held everything in common; they would sell their property and possessions and make a general distribution as the need of each required. With one mind they kept up their daily attendance at the temple, and, breaking bread in private houses, shared their meals with unaffected joy, as they praised God. (Acts 2, 46—47).

This prototype of a Christian community has found a living expression throughout the centuries in the monastic tradition which preserves a genuine importance. The community of Taizé is an excellent example. But today, at a time of fundamental transformation of consciousness and the corresponding social order, new models are imperative in all spheres of life, in our work as well as in public life. There is an urgent need to dare to experiment with new types of communities and new ways of living the healing ministry of the Church. However, the new, to be true, has to be related to tradition in such a way that it makes us more deeply aware of the universal truth which in different epochs of development has found expression in different forms.

I would like to conclude these comments on our corporate witness with a vision of the healing church as seen by Roger Schutz, the prior of the Taizé community.

The Risen Christ comes to quicken a festival in the innermost heart of man. He is preparing a spring time of the Church: a Church devoid of means of power, ready to share with all a place of visible communion for all humanity. He is going to give us enough imagination and courage to open up a path of reconciliation. He is going to prepare us to give our life so that man will be no longer victim of man. (Letter from Taizé "Preparing the Council of Young People", May 1970).

V.

These words bring us back to the theme of reconciliation. The Healing Church in its deepest meaning must be a place of understanding, of forgiveness and of reconciliation.

A French proverb says: "to understand all is to forgive all." There is a great truth in this. I must be able to penetrate to the depth of myself as well as of my neighbour to get the kind of understanding which enables me to forgive. Such forgiveness is rooted in being united in Christ and through him with my neighbour, enabling me to "love my enemies". Such love, which is different from a condescending attitude towards other people, presupposes an inner transformation, a transcendence of the realm of the opposites freeing us to move into the realm of the polarities where we can find our true self. This is a precondition of

92

true reconciliation.

Unitey in Christ, being a member of the healing Church or centredness in our own true self which relates us to the centre of the universe, are but different ways of speaking about the same phenomenon. They are manifestations of our relatedness to the universal cosmic Christ, who calls us with these words: "Dwell in me, as I in you. No branch can bear fruit of itself, but only if it remains united with the vine; no more can you bear fruit, unless you remain united with me. (John 15, 4).

To be united with Christ is the most transforming healing experience which in its deepest expression means "to be born again". In Jesus' words:—

In truth I tell you, no one can enter the kingdom of God without being born from water and spirit ... You ought not to be astonished then, when I tell you that you must be born over again. The wind blows where it wills; you hear the sound of it, you do not know where it comes from, or where it is going. So with everyone who is born from spirit. (John 3, 5—8).

Footnotes:

1. A Chassid Saying from Israel ben Eliezer, the Baal Shem Tov 1700—1760

2. Friedrich Heer, *Gottes erste Liebe,* Bechtle Verlag 1967, p.7

3. W.D. Wendland, *Die Kirche in der modernen Gesell-schaft,* Hamburg 1958, pp.127—128

Chapter 4

THE WOUNDED HEALER*

I.

As we have just seen, true healing implies a transformation which in its ultimate meaning is equivalent to being twice-born. In this chapter we shall explore in greater depth a question which we have mentioned so far only incidentally, namely, how the person to be healed and the person who is an instrument of healing are interrelated in the healing process. More specifically we are concerned with the implications of being wounded and being able to carry the wounds of others.

We do not usually think of a healer as wounded. Our customary way of thinking is to consider the person who heals as a healthy person and the person to be healed as the one who has been wounded. Without denying the obvious element of truth in such a conception, we must beware of the risk of an oversimplification which obscures some of the deeper aspects of the relationship between being wounded, healing and being healed.

To understand the complexity of the issues raised once we recognize their interrelationship a simple analogy may be helpful. I am ill and have fever. The doctor comes and gives me a medication. The fever disappears. Did the medication heal me? Or did I become healthy as a result of forces in my body which restored the balance which had been disturbed and hence led to my having fever?

* This is a slightly modified version of a talk given at two conferences of L'Arche in France in 1980 and 1982.

Did my relationship to the doctor also have an influence on my overcoming the illness? To pose these questions is sufficient to show that the healing process may be a complex one—even in the case of a relatively simple illness of the body. A disturbance of the balance of our psyche is a much more intricate phenonenon which has many ramifications and touches manifold relationships. In our explorations of the wounded healer we are basically concerned with relationships to our-selves, to others, and to a deeper reality of life understood as interrelated phenomena, not as three separate aspects of our being.

II.

The quality of relationship which is a precondition for healing to take place is a relationship of empathy. To have empathy means to have the ability to grasp the inner world of another person in a feeling-intuitive way. This capacity is, in turn, closely related to our own personal experience. It would be wrong to say categorically that we can only have empathy for another person if we have already experienced what the other person is experiencing. Our own experience becomes wider and deeper as we meet new situations. But there are limits to our understanding and our capacity to experience. In this sense our empathy is limited by our potentiality for participating in the experience of another person.

To have empathy with a person who has been wounded presupposes that we ourselves know in some way what it means to be wounded. But to help another person to be healed we must not only have empathy; we must also be able to express our empathy through an unconditional "acceptance" and patient support of the process of growth of the other person. To be real these attitudes must, as already mentioned in Chapter 1, have the spontaneity of love. St. Paul has given us the best description of the meaning of true love:

> *Love is patient; love is kind and envies no one. Love is never boastful, nor conceited, nor rude; never selfish, not quick to take offence. Love keeps no score of wrongs; does not gloat over other men's sins, but delights in the truth. There is nothing love cannot face; there is no limit to its faith, its hope, and its endurance.* (1 Cor. 13, 4—7)

Such love cannot be artificially created. It cannot be demanded but can only be freely given out of a living relationship to the source of all life. It wells up, so to speak, spontaneously from the Source which is immanent in our inmost being, alive at our centre. At the same time it transcends the boundaries of our bodies just, as in the following dream, stars spark from the centre into the universe.

> *I am searching for my centre . . . I find silver stars. I am searching for the boundaries of my body. As I do this, stars spark from my centre into the universe.*

This dream symbolizes the unity of the true centre of a person and a transpersonal centre. For true healing to take place, we must be related to a centre, to a source from which healing energy — that is love — emanates. Since "there is no greater love than this, that a man should lay down his life for his friends" (John 15, 14). Jesus of Nazareth embodies the deepest love alive at our centre. He pointed to the ultimate source of this love when he said: "I am not myself the source of the words I speak to you: it is the Father who dwells in me doing his own work." (John 14,

10). The energy emanating from this source is the energy of transformation. Its essential quality is expressed in "Behold! I am making all things new!" (Revelation 21, 5). The power to make all things new is the fundamental power to heal. Ultimately nameless, this power comes alive in different ways. In the following dream it is symbolized by an archbishop:

> The Archbishop comes to my house. I realize that there is something negative in me, something that has to be lifted up. Then a circle forms itself around me—the archbishop, my children, my husband. They invite me to a full life.

Here is the archbishop, symbol of the true universal Church, of the Spirit, of Christ who initiates, so to speak, the formation of a circle around this deeply wounded person. The circle has, as mentioned in Chapter 1, the meaning of a *temenos,* a protective yet open circle which every child needs to grow up healthily. It also has the meaning of perfection or completion. It expresses the full-ness, the wholeness of life. It is a symbol of the divine.

The search for the healing power at the centre is also expressed in a dream in which a person surrounded by "animated beings"—symbolizing creation—becomes aware of the need to have a living relationship to her centre. It is significant that this dream repeated itself in the same night, a rather rare occurrence which shows the importance of its message. When mediating on this dream, the dreamer had a sudden realization that "what matters is not Jesus two thousand years ago, but Jesus in the present." The dream gave an experience of a Presence which made the person feel "free, full of life for the rest of the day, but later this feeling petered out." This experience illustrates the source of transformation. But it also shows the problem of healing: to establish a relationship to the Centre which is alive and does not peter out. We must become centred in such a way that our relationship to the Source *spontaneously* expresses our true self.

III.

In order to understand more clearly the way in which the transforming energy emanating from the Source affects the healing process we must look more closely at the relationship between the wound, the one who helps the healing process and the one who needs to be healed. I have intentionally avoided the words "healer" and "patient" or "ill person" because the relationship which we want to understand is in fact much more complex.

In classical psycho-analysis, the relationship between the analyst and the patient is understood in terms of the transference. This means that the patient "transfers" onto the analyst aspects of his inner experience as if he had experienced it—or was experiencing it now—with the analyst. For example: the patient experiences the analyst as if he or she were his father, mother or brother. There is no doubt that transference is an important aspect of a relationship in which a deep wound needs to be healed. It is indeed an aspect of every human relationship in which we project something onto another person that is actually alive within us. The phenomenon of transference must, therefore, be understood properly and taken seriously. But the transference relationship does not itself contain the power of transformation as already mentioned in Chapter 1. That power is activated when two human beings meet at depth—that is at their centres.

The diagram on page 100 illustrates such a relationship. The circle on the left hand side represents the person whom we ordinarily consider the healer. Actually he or she is the somehow wounded person who helps the healing process. We shall, therefore, refer to him/her as the wounded healer. The circle on the right hand represents the person whom we usually consider to be ill but who in fact is not only the wounded one but also has in himself or herself an "inner" healer. Healing takes place as the wounded healer and the person to be healed enter into a relationship at depth, activating the centre which is the gateway to the Source of transformation.

To be wounded means to be somehow cut off from the Source. The essence of the healing process consists in opening up the way to the Source by removing whatever obstacles, blocks or defences interfere with the free flow of the ever-renewing, transforming energy. Having been wounded helps the "wounded healer" to establish the kind of relationship of understanding and acceptance which fosters this process.

At the beginning of the healing process the wounded healer usually has to "carry" the wound of the person to be healed, that is he or she has to accept all the negative manifestations of a wound—hatred, anger, resentment— without experiencing these as directed against him or herself. At the same time the wounded healer has to "carry" through empathy the pain, the suffering caused by the wound. In so doing the wounded healer affirms the true self alive at the centre but not yet accessible to the person to be healed because obstacles interfere with the free access. We may also say that the wounded healer takes upon him or herself the pain and the suffering, as well as the negative reactions, of the other person. But this is only genuine if this happens at that centre of the wounded

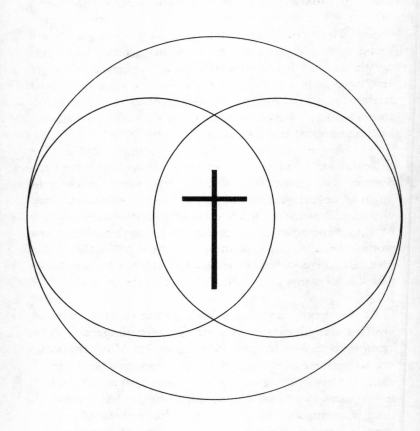

healer at which a transpersonal reality is touched. Unless this is the case, the taking-upon-oneself of the suffering of the other is in danger of being a masochistic act rather than an expression of a true trinitarian human relationship.

The transpersonal centre which is touched in the wounded healer and activated in the person to be healed is represented on page 100 by the midpoint of the larger circle that surrounds the two circles representing the wounded healer and the person to be healed. This larger circle is as shown on page 100, interwoven with their personal centres and with the totality of their being: our inmost, our centre is the "reference point" of our "wholeness" just as the midpoint of a circle is the "reference point" of its circumference. There is no circle without a midpoint and the midpoint belongs to the circle. In this sense the transpersonal centre is interwoven with the centre and totality of the wounded healer and the person to be healed. The cross, symbol of the interpenetration of the horizontal and the vertical, of the earth and of heaven, marks the transpersonal Centre which ultimately carries the wound.

As we already mentioned, only through a living relationship to that deeper reality of life which is alive at the transpersonal Centre can the wounded healer truly carry the wound in a way which can free the person to be healed from the obstacles cutting him or her off from the centre. When such a relationship is established, the healing power alive in the person to be healed can be freed step by step. In that sense the person to be healed is also a healer. The loving acceptance of the wound, first by the wounded healer and later by the person to be healed, or rather of the wholeness of the person to be healed, thus initiates a process of renewal which, in its ultimate manifestation, is an experience of rebirth. Just as the Cross and the Resurrection are inseparable, so the acceptance of the wound and the freeing of the transforming energy are inseparable. In this sense it is the reality of the Cross and Resurrection which is the ultimate power of transformation underlying the healing process.

The depth of pain which a person may experience is expressed in this dream:

> *I am forced to look at a torture scene. There is a man and a woman . . . a gun is put through them as if through a hole in their stomach up to the mouth. I wake up at the limit of pain . . .*

Not much needs to be said to indicate the depth of the wound and of the suffering of the person who had this dream.

Another dream illustrates the healing process:

> *I am sitting at a long table. A healer is behind me. He touches my head with his thumb. Then a lapis-lazuli sprang from the top of my head. I touched my head and found what seemed to be a hole. It hurt and the wound bled but I know that it will heal . . .*

In this dream a healer appears explicitly. He emerges from a reality hitherto unconscious (he appears behind the person to be healed) and simply touches the head (the centre of all the energy centres in our body) with his finger. This touches off the precious stone which springs from the head as, in the myth, Minerva sprang from the head of Zeus. When this happens, there comes an awareness of the wound, previously hidden, and at the same time a knowledge of transformation.

In the prophecies of Isaiah announcing Israel as "a

Light to the Nations" a *lapis lazuli* becomes the foundation of a city which was "storm-battered . . . distressed and disconsolate" but which shall now be freed after the servant of man has appeared; the man who was "pierced for our transgressions, tortured for our iniquities . . . Yet the Lord took thought for his tortured servant and healed him who had made himself a sacrifice for sin." (Isaiah 53).

The sequence of events in this Biblical account is analogous to essential aspects of the healing process: healing takes place through an acceptance of suffering. Such an acceptance, which, in its deepest expression is love, must take place within the wounded healer as well as within the person to be healed. This is well illustrated in the following dream:

There is a deeply hurt child. I take her and adopt her into our family. She will fit though she is hurt. We adopt the child into our family and then we realize how much more hurt the child is than we know. We must love her. I take her into my arms . . .

The child to be adopted is the wounded inner child of the person to be healed who had indeed a deep, all-pervading injury from early childhood. The depth of this wound was hidden until now. But at the moment of consciousness, when she is taking responsibility for her own wounds (the child is adopted into the family), the real wound becomes apparent. To be healed the hurt child needs love, for only love can release the transforming energy which heals.

This process of transformation is usually accompanied by a struggle between "good and evil" within us. The power of light and hope has to struggle with the powers of darkness, of fear and doubt. The Hebrew word for the

103

devil is "the one who comes in-between", that is the energy which cuts us off from the Source of Life, the powers which block its free flow. As these powers come alive in us—and they are bound to come alive whenever we are not affirmed in our true self, our centre—we must defend ourselves against the onslaught of the forces of evil by building protective walls or other more elaborate structures—as mentioned in Chapter 2. This is illustrated in the following dream:

I am riding a pony. It collapses, becomes quite small, lies down on a bed and sleeps. I am in a room which has no windows. It is built of red bricks. I hear a noise and the wall collapses. Everything collapses around me. It was a nightmare.

It is indeed frightening if both the vital energy which carried us (the pony) and the room which gave us whatever security we were able to muster, collapse. Life in a dark room may not have been very pleasant but, in this case, it was at least safe and protected this person from the negative forces unleashed by the injury.

If we suffer an injury early in our life, the activation of negative forces is unavoidable. The child at a certain stage of development is subject to the law of "an eye for an eye and a tooth for a tooth." This means that the denial of affirmation and love, which is the root cause of all wounds, automatically activates negative counterforces. Though this happens without the child's volition being involved, the child has a sense of guilt which in some cases can be crippling. When this happens, it is difficult for the person who needs to be healed to experience the loving acceptance by the wounded healer—or rather by that reality of which the wounded healer is an instrument.

There may indeed be many obstacles which have to be overcome before the person to be healed is open to the healing energies within himself or herself. Their activation in the relationship to the wounded healer often needs a good deal of time. The following dream illustrates inner forces which have to be overcome before the power of transformation can be freed:

> My husband and I invite you to our house. You are there. Then a woman comes. She takes possession of you and you leave with her.

This dream could signify that there is something in the "wounded healer" that interferes with the healing process. It could also mean that the person who helps the healing process symbolizes the true self—the essential centre—of the person to be healed. The dream would then indicate the inner forces (symbolised in the woman who takes possession of the healer) with which this person has to struggle in order to be open to the Source of transformation.

These examples may suffice to show that the person who is an instrument for activating the healing power is interrelated with the person who has the wound in a way which allows the power of transformation alive at the Centre—and hence at the centre of each person—to be freed. Both need patience, both must take responsibility for the wound and for its consequences, both must suffer in the spirit of that love which St. Paul described so movingly.

IV.

Ultimately all life has a mysterious quality. Why is one person wounded and another not, or at least not as deeply, though the circumstances seem to be similar? Why can the healing process be activated only slowly in some situations and much faster in others, though the injuries do not seem to be very different? Why are the resentment and the negative feelings aroused by the wound difficult to overcome in one situation and much easier in another? The significance of these questions for our theme becomes apparent as we listen a third time to St. Paul:

> *The wound which is borne in God's way brings a change of heart too salutary to regret; but the hurt which is borne in the world's way brings death.* (2 Cor. 7, 10).

The wound which is borne in God's way is a wound which is accepted without resentment and negative feelings. The hurt which is borne in the world's way evokes resentment and hatred, often hatred of oneself which is as destructive as hatred of others; indeed they have the same source, only the direction of their manifestation is different.

To speak in the language of the dream about the child to be adopted, healing means to bear the wound in God's way by taking the wounded child into our home, in our arms, and give it love. This love, like all true love, is not a sentimental outpouring of emotions but in this case implies an acceptance of our destiny. It means that whatever may have happened to us, we can say in our inmost being: "Here I am." This is a new day, a gift of life." Thank you my Lord." Why this injury happened to me and not to someone else is an unanswerable question. It remains part of the mystery. We must not avoid this query but we must leave the answer in God's hands. This, like Job, we can do only if we experience the transcending majesty of God; if we experience a reality which transcends the contradictions of human experience, if we penetrate to and are penetrated by that light which shines forth in the One who could say "I am the Light of the World."

The interaction of our conscious effort to grasp this light and the spontaneous un-called for emergence of this light is another aspect of healing which has a mysterious quality. This is the mystery of the interaction of our will and God's grace. I illustrate this by another dream:

I must build a bridge. I was at the shore of a wide river, about half a mile wide. First I could not see the other side of the river. Then I became aware that there was land on the other side. A voice told me; you must build a bridge. My immediate idea was to build a bridge quite high, supported by many pillars. But a man said: "No, you must build the bridge with one span." I felt this was good.

This dream shows the importance of an initiative. The dreamer had to build that bridge herself, but the voice who initiated the idea came from the Source which contained the energy necessary to build the bridge—and to do it in one determined action. Will-power and grace, activity and passivity, transformation and acceptance, thrust and receptivity are thus interrelated and interact when the wounded healer and the person to be healed meet at the Centre. This is the way to the transforming power alive at the Source and incarnated in Jesus as the Christ.

In Him we find indeed the deepest and ultimate manifestation of the wounded healer, namely, the One who though not wounded himself, has such a depth of relatedness to all life that he can take the wounds of others upon himself. A person struggling to bear her own wounds in this spirit had the following dream:

> *An owl gives up the protection of the trees. It gives up its power to catch mice and walks, its wings hanging down, in the open field to the river. I have the impression of a positive passivity.*

The person who had this dream felt that it was related to the Passion. It is indeed a symbol of giving up one's power of destruction—to "Put up your sword" (Matth., 26, 52)—to find renewal in the water of Life. The "passivity" is positive because it transcends the opposites of passivity and activity in the mystery of a transcendent union.

Jesus of Nazareth may be said to have been "passive" in undergoing the Passion. But he was at the same time "active" in a twofold sense. Moving towards God with the thrust of his whole being, he was deeply related to the divine reality. At the same time he was so deeply related to humankind, indeed to the very people who crucified him, that he could take the sins of others upon himself. To be able to do so he must have penetrated to the inmost core of those who killed him, beyond the very wounds and barriers which separated them from their own true selves. He was thus most actively related to them at that centre which is also the Centre of the Universe.

In its deepest meaning, to be the wounded healer means to be able to enter into the mystery of the Passion. It means to experience in ourselves that another human being has taken our wounds upon him/herself to the limit of giving his/her life for us, thus affirming what is most beautiful and most true in us. If we can enter into this event, we participate in the power of transformation which

108

manifested itself in Jesus of Nazareth 2000 years ago and in the living Christ every day. This participation enables us too to take upon ourselves the wounds of others and to be in this deepest and ultimate sense "the wounded healer."

Chapter 5

HEALING A WOUND — AN EXPERIENCE

This theme is closely related to that of the preceding chapter, not simply because Ruth, the person with whom we are concerned, came to work with me after having become acquainted with that material, but also because it illustrates the implications and results of the approach outlined in "The Wounded Healer".

The work described in this chapter started with three exploratory sessions followed by a week in residence. The flexibility of such a setting made it possible to carry through an integrated approach bringing together meditation, exploration of dreams, guided inner journeys, drawing and related approaches.

I.

Ruth is a deeply religious person, now in her mid-forties, who decided at the age of 16 to become a nun and who took her last vows when she was 22 years old. She is a warm, soft-spoken but strong woman.

Her main complaint was fear: "It prevents me from talking in public. It makes me use all my energy to run away from things I'm afraid of doing. It makes me feel I really can't do them. When I was in London I literally ran away from tables where some of the speakers shared the meal. At home, at some public meetings my fear is so great that I cannot take my place. I know I should contribute something but I can't and I don't. So I come out of the meeting more afraid and guilty because I did not voice my opinion or take a stand—so I try to evade the next meeting . . ."

During the first exploratory session which we had, she presented me with a drawing entitled "My wound"; at the bottom, slightly to the right of the centre was a red circle pierced by a strong dark vibrating line which was surrounded by a spiral movement opening slightly towards the top towards a background of wider red and dark lines making a swirling movement. The whole drawing was imbued by a strong energy alive in every line.

The questions and comments which accompanied this drawing were:

"What was I born for?
I want to talk to you about my place.
I just want to continue to listen to where I am and only from there move on.
I want to listen to the voice that says 'My grace is all you need'.
I feel I would need a great deal of time in silence and prayer to find myself, God and others.
I still can't hold on to anything."

After the first exploratory session, she climbed a mountain with a friend in the afternoon. She gave the following account of her experiences which reveal the same characteristics as her first drawing, namely a wound manifesting itself in fear. On her way up she had to walk on a narrow path hewn into a deeply sloping mountain

"suspended over a hole,
a green slope dotted with rocks,

111

a few trees to stop one's fall in some areas but mostly an
   open stretch down.
My head turns
— some power pulls it down in a rotating swing.
My guts contract: fear fills my viscera,
fear of that abyss, endless, leading to a fast death.
Fear and attraction, deathly attraction cohabit, co-
   dwell in me.
Strange combination.
My hand, my heart reach for a strong hold,
reach for a rock
— hold the rock —
caress it
— touch it with a total touch . . .
A Presence comes through a hand,
a warm hand,
a heart in a hand,
an extension of life,
an invitation to life, warmth, presence.
Something, someone to hold on to.
Life-death all at once.
All in a fleeting moment . . ."

After the second exploratory session, Ruth went on
another excursion which gave her an opportunity to go
with a group early in the morning to watch the sunrise
from a mountain top. Arriving at the mountain top Ruth
met life in its fullness:

"My heart bounces in plenitude.
The peak stood against a sky of light —
a light from a source hidden, wide and deep like an
   ocean . . .
Great waves of light swelled up.
My heart touches the light —
and the warmth of my own source and depth . . .

Like a child coming out of the womb, the sun breaks
   out.
Dances the light.
My whole body and soul is touched . . .
Death: the entry,
Death: the light.
Death: the total presence and union — forever."

The experience of death too is twofold — as the abyss
and as the gateway to life eternal. This dual meaning
reveals an inner reality stretching from the fear of nothingness to a cosmic rapture and union with all of humankind
in the Godhead.

These two ingredients of life and death were quite
concreteley acted out later on the same excursion in a

"dangerous slide down on a melting glacier."
"In the swing and speed I lay transported, present,
   carried by some energy, surrendering to it:
in trust I lay, peaceful and present and moving fast like
   a feather in the air.
The friction of the snow increased the speed of the
   descent —
a moment of total living, pure, non-controlled, letting
   go to the forces of life.
— Early morning it was, fresh and cool.
My hands rubbed against the icy snow, my legs outstretched for greater freedom.
The world was upside down and my heart free.
A moment of trust.
Just a few seconds!
One bubble of Life!
One whole!
me breathing - free!
there in one moment!"

Returning from this excursion, Ruth drew the

"trail leading to the top"

showing the perilous path, the abyss and a dark hole. She also did a drawing

"My heart",

showing four ovals arranged like the leaves of a flower pointing towards the four corners of the earth. At the centre is a red point, the leaves are red surrounded by a bright yellow. This flower form is above the top of a mountain range, dwarfing these mountains to a fraction of their size. This drawing was in fact a mandala—symbolic expression of a beautiful and harmonious deeper reality of life alive in her and expressed in

"the moment of total living"

and the

"moment of trust".

It indicated the ability to transcend the ambiguity of the

"death wish"

and to become open to the healing power of a divine Presence.

As we talked about these experience, Ruth was reminded of an event which happened when she was four years old:

"I had found out in a cupboard at home, on a top shelf, that my next Christmas gift was a doll and I did not

want to play with dolls any more because I did not find interest and pleasure in dolls any more. I thought that my mother should˜know that and that if she bought the doll it meant she did not know me, she did not know where I was, what I liked . . . So I decided that from now on I would have to be by myself, to carry my own things inside."

The gift of a doll to a girl four years of age in itself could not have marked a watershed in the life of a child if it had not been symptomatic of a deep sense (Freud would have called it a screen memory)

"mother does not know me and hence does not truly love me."

For many people an experience of this kind would have meant a rupture not only with the actual parent but with the divine reality, with a nourishing, loving God. Ruth, however, was able to turn towards the living God who gave her sustenance and life; but being human, subject to the laws of human growth and development, a deep wound was inflicted on her, a wound that remained, a wound of not-being-known, not-being-loved, being alone and confronted with forces that are infinitely greater than ours and hence arouse great fear.

We parted after three days during which we had three sessions and a shared silent meditation. She responded with reservation to my invitation to spend a longer time of exploration at a later date, yet with a hidden joy

"for the invitation corresponds to something inside that feels and knows this is the direction of life, growth, opening, destiny . . ."

Later, when looking back to this time she said

*"I was overwhelmed to be extended such an invitation —
It touched me in the same way as I am touched by God's
ways with me:
—I felt that it was an act of grace."*

II.

When Ruth arrived about six weeks later she brought with
her two drawings. One showed a mountain landscape,
majestic, almost overwhelming. The predominant colours
were grey, a deep blue, and black with some deep green
trees. A path led to an opening similar to a cave near the
bottom of the landscape. Yellow light radiated from this
cave — a patch of light coming from the depth of the
mountain and illuminating the foreground. She described
this drawing as

"The Cavern Where the Lamb Waits"

expressing a

*"longing for silence, hiding, being with, close to the love
inside me."*

Here again is a dual experience of hiding from and being
close — an experience of the womb as containing and as
life-giving. The love inside her is symbolized by the Lamb
of God, by Jesus taking upon himself the suffering of humankind. Ruth did not say this and I did not interpret it this
way either at the time.

The second drawing showed a white centre, forming an

116

inner circle surrounded by a firework-like outburst of fine red lines moving out in all directions and forming an uneven circular pattern. She gave to this drawing the name

"Accept".

Her comment was:

"When I drew this I was hurting all over like most of the time during the past months. While doing the drawing and when looking at it afterwards I felt that saying 'yes' to the red and to the hurt would bring some healing, thus the title to "accept".

The inner movement expressed in these drawings illustrates an important aspect of all healing: the acceptance of the wound without resentment. As long as we are resentful we are caught deep down in a vicious circle of powerlessness, countervailing aggression and/or hatred combined with guilt. In order to be able to free ourselves from such an encirclement we must have access to an energy with a transcending power, an energy which can lift us out of our caughtness, thus opening a way towards inner freedom. For Ruth this power of transformation was alive in her relationship to Jesus and to God — the rock on which she built her life.

This is clearly expressed in the way in which she had summed up her experiences during the final days before coming to work with me:

"I want to continue to work at liberating myself of so many 'blockages' —
free myself — choose God again.
This means to listen to His voice, to the spirit inside:
to be faithful now where I am, in what I see and hear.

When I go through a change, I seem to lose track of His
    Face—
and I need to find Him again in my new place—
with new eyes—find His contour in my heart.
Jesus, who are you?
Where are you?
I feel you are so present here, now—yet I am so far
    from you.
To choose Jesus again means to receive his new light,
to open to his voice inside me as I hear it now,
to surrender to his movement in me.
I am unable to initiate that.
Jesus is always initiating, inviting, loving.
I can only yearn, call for Him to come to me.
I desire to be 'well' in my total, radical poverty.
I desire to stand in a group sharing my gift and my
    poverty.
I want to be faithful to Jesus, my Love.
Today I look frequently at Jesus to offer myself,
to ask him to teach me how to love others . . ."

She was free to question everything because somehow
deep down she had the security of the knowledge of the
reality of Jesus who through the acceptance of suffering
and pain could free the power of transformation and
transcendence. The secret of what happened subsequently
was the way Ruth bore her wound. In the words of St.
Paul:

"For the wound which is borne in God's way brings a
change of heart too salutary to regret; but the hurt
which is borne in the world's way brings death. You
bore your hurt in God's way and see what the results
have been." (2 Cor., 7, 10—11).

III.

Filled with a deep desire "to find my call and to live it fully and to find unity", Ruth started to work with me, first with a meditative exercise with which I became familiar through my work with Raihanna, a Sufi mystic in India. Raihanna had introduced me to this exercise by saying that she gives it different names depending upon the religious convictions of the person and that, for me, she would call it "Receiving the Sacrament". The actual exercise is quite simple. It begins with the person standing in order to give the greatest possible freedom of action. To start sitting makes it necessary to get up before we can move, but standing we can directly move into any posture or position we are led to take. Standing—and having a substantial free space around us in which we can move— the exercise begins with concentrating on what the person is aware of at the moment, the deepest experience of his/her life. There are not specific expectations of what may happen; the person is free to be silent, to talk, to remain standing or to move—and to act in whatever way she or he "feels like".

Ruth summed up her experience during this meditative exercise by saying that "I feel like a lump—no shape—no angles—nothing where I can be grabbed"—"I feel unloved . . . I am reminded of my experience when I was four years old." These are not the kind of experiences which we would expect from a meditative exercise. Yet I had similarly surprising results when doing this exercise with other people. For reasons I cannot explain clearly, this exercise touches something very deep that has to be explored, understood and worked through before the person can live "wholly" from his or her spiritual centre.

Ruth discovered a lump—something, as she said herself,

that was unformed yet contained a great deal of power which was arrested and which blocked the flow of the spiritual energy. Since the experience of herself as a lump came alive in the same space of time as the re-collection of her experience as a four year old girl, she revealed an inner connection between these two experiences. It is as if she "had" a lump in her throat or chest — or any part of her body — which was due to the denial of love and the withdrawal from relationship, and which impeded her breath — symbol of the incarnation of the divine. This was indeed Ruth's situation: her relationship to God and to Jesus was essentially unimpaired. But her ability to live the reality of Christ in her self-awareness and her human relationships was injured.

Overlapping the experience touched off by the meditative exercise, Ruth had an experience which aroused deep fear in her, namely an invitation to visit with me and my family, a friend who held in high position in the Church of England. It is not possible to say to what extent the activation of this fear was directly related to this exercise and to what extent it was primarily or even exclusively the result of this invitation. I said that she did not have to come but suggested that she use this visit to "look at" her fear, to live it by observing it and sharing it with me. This led to a clarification of the way the fear manifested itself, starting with the fear of learning to swim and her inability to swim in deep water, and showing itself in the various ways already mentioned above.

The fear of swimming in deep water is symbolic of a fear of what we usually call "the unconscious" and what actually represents the energies alive in a deeper reality of life. At the same time as Ruth re-experienced the fear of her life, a deep longing came alive in her: "to be free . . . to say what I have to say without fear, spontaneously and in simplicity; not to feel that things depend on me only; not to feel that I have always to know and give the right answers; to be sitting beside other people having other gifts and being OK . . ." These words express a deep desire to free the access to the source of life—and thus be able to be spontaneous—spontaneity, as mentioned in Chapter 1, being an expression of a living relationship to a deeper order and truth. It also expresses a desire not to demand an impossible perfection from herself and not to be threatened by the gifts and potentialities of others. There is a true striving for perfection in the sense of striving to realize the deepest and highest in us. There is also a false striving for perfection—a need which arises when a child feels unlovable, only able to gain love through performing good deeds, thus becoming "perfect". This is the need for perfection from which Ruth wanted to be free.

The first response to facing the fear was despair: "I'm stuck! I don't believe I can get rid of that powerful fear. I'm giving up in a way. Perhaps I should just live with it." The despair was expressed in a drawing which she entitled "The Wheel". It was a circle almost totally black at the circumference and becoming lighter towards the centre. Her comments were: "The wheel crushes me. I can't break it, it is too powerful. I can't smash it. It controls me. It is stronger than me. That fear makes me unreasonable. I let myself be paralysed by it. I get trapped in its movement."

After having faced the crushing fear, Ruth first raised some questions about the meaning of her coming to work with me, questioning what I could do and wondering how she could "find her destiny". Out of these questions came further reflections: "I touch a new peace. I worry less about finding my place, about why I am here: some 'slow cooking' is taking place inside, some ripening, some change, growth, a quiet and slow process but as sure as the slow growth from flower to fruit in a plant. It is now OK for me to stay and wait and not act—and just to be. I feel I have been loved enough, told enough that I am loved, that I must

go on . . ."

This was combined with a sense

"of a deep joy"

of meditating with me and a thankfulness for the time I spend with her

"listening and answering my questions.
A desire rises to be faithful not with my will but quietly,
*   softly in my heart,*
to be open to the gift of the moment with all my heart,
to let things happen slowly."

She was puzzled why

"in this gratefulness I am not enthusiastic as I often was before"

explaining it in these words:

"I have touched my poverty, the impossibility of doing anything for myself and this experience seems to balance, to keep down excessive joy or other positive emotions. And I also know that this state of darkness can be just around the corner and I like to prepare for the coming of Jesus in that way."

122

IV.

Ruth decided to come along to visit my friend. In the first exploration after our arrival at my friend's house, she expressed an experience of

"something is melting in me.
I don't know exactly what it is . . .
I am in a rotten place.
I would like to disappear . . .
I don't know where I am, where I should go, but I want to go to the truth . . .
I feel mad for having made that decision when I was 4 years old.
I also feel sad about it.
Why cut myself off from care?"

While sensing new life—a melting of the frozen layers of pain—Ruth was also becoming free to face her pain in a new way. The agony of her wound was reflected in a drawing which shows her in an empty room without windows and the door closed. She is kneeling at a wall, her hands—almost twice as elongated as outstretched hands actually would be—touching the bare wall.

"My hands are outstretched—they know the wall.
They know every bump on the wall.
I have touched that pain before.
I know it.
I know it so well.
I can feel every contour of it . . .
Does every human being have to live such pain?
In one form or another?"

When we next talked together she told me the following dream which she had the night before:

123

"A friend of mine, a very talented, successful, intuitive therapist, in the course of a session with a group of approximately ten people, is inviting each participant to do something he or she can really do well. He comes to me and says 'You draw a baby living in solitude. I'm sure you can do it well.' I feel the exercise is appropriate for me — that in fact, he again is right on, he is connecting to me, he knows what to ask me. A flash comes to my mind 'How can one tell of the solitude of a baby with pink and blue colours as are ordinarily used for baby boys and girls? On the other hand, it can't be the colour of 'Rosemary's' black baby carriage.' Here I remembered a movie 'Rosemary's Baby' where we see a big black carriage, wholly covered with black material from the top of it to the side hangings right down to the floor and where we never see the body."

This dream does not need an elaborate interpretation. It speaks for itself, revealing the essence of her wound:

"a baby living in solitude".

No wonder it is not possible to imagine such a baby clad in blue or pink — only a carriage covered from top to bottom with blackness and no baby visible at all would be an appropriate image. But in fact the situation transcends human imagination — hence it

"can't be the colour of Rosemary's black baby carriage."

A baby — in solitude — can't truly be.

We, as adults, may visualize a baby lying in a carriage alone for a while in a nicely furnished room while its mother is absent working elsewhere in or out of the house. Yet for the baby the experience is totally different from

124

the situation just described. It is of a cosmic nature: abandoned in the darkness of infinite space and endless time, a human being who is still embedded in the world of Mother and not yet able to live without resting in an invisible but absolutely real circle of light and care, is torn from the life-giving womb of emotional embeddedness and security and thrown into the abyss of nothingness. In such a "dark hole" all the wild animals, witches and devils alive in fairy tales appear endowed with a power compared to which we are as helpless as a fly on a table, about to be killed by the incomparable might of the blow of a fist. For a baby such overwhelming power is invested in the parents who are endowed with a divine aura. This is why I spelled "Mother" with a capital "M"—in order to indicate that the baby cannot differentiate between the actual parents and a deeper reality of life which endows the parental figures of flesh and blood with a power of a transpersonal, universal, archetypal nature.

The memory of the four year old girl, deciding to "go it alone" because her mother gave her a doll in which she was no longer interested, finds a real meaning in this dream. It was the only dream she had during the week we worked together—except for the recollection of a dream which she had twenty years ago to which I will come back later. The dream of the baby abandoned in solitude brought back the experience of the lump—just as in our first meditative exercise the experience of herself as a lump and the memory of the four year old girl were linked.

"Today" she said, "the lump hurts wherever you touch it. I cry and very often ask if you are there. I need you being there with me. I can't go there alone . . ." This shows the vital significance of a human relationship to meet the wounds inflicted on us. Being human we need another human being to be able to descend into the abyss of darkness and to face a pain too great to take form and hence hidden in the lump. Feeling this hurt Ruth remembered moments in her life when she felt this primordial experience of eternal solitude so strongly that physical symptoms appeared. "When cut off in my relationships with people in . . . I suffered from a lung disease. When I was small and I felt cut off, at two years old, at seven and at nineteen, I suffered from pneumonia. With people I love and who care for me, I have a 'heart to heart' contact. The only calm and comfort for me, where I get most rest in pain, what I want most, is this real contact with someone. Is this the search for what I missed when I was younger?"

V.

The next morning Ruth told me that the lump had been flattened and showed me a drawing of a flat form—it could have been almost anything—outlined by a fairly straight, though undulated line at the top and even more strongly undulating lower part. The effect was something akin to a half circle. There were some wavy lines and quite a few dots on the surface of this form which was drawn in a perspective that indicated a thickness of about a quarter of an inch. "It looks like a pancake", she said, "I feel no motivation and am afraid. I am not stuck, I am blank—flat like a pancake. When a pancake is frying it rises in bubbles of air that lift up the dough, then just fall flat again in the pan. This is what the lines across the drawing are saying. There is not use working with you. I am getting nowhere. All I find and uncover is layer after layer of negative things, an endless bottomless collection. I am afraid of staying in this place forever: no base to live from. Do you know where I am going?"

These words of despair were complemented by another drawing which is difficult to describe. It looked somehow like a junkyard dominated by an enormous open tin whose cover pointed to heaven like an oval signpost. "The drawing" she said, "can only show the top of a heap of refuse accumulated through the years in that dump. I feel that this junkyard is inside me: layer after layer of negative things. With these words she intuited what had to be worked through at a later stage of our work together—and she expressed the horror of a pain which is "endless" in time and "bottomless" in space—thus transcending the space-time of human experience and leaving us without a "base"—the ground of our being undermined. In this lies its cosmic character and its superhuman power. I pointed this out to her and answered her query with some words of reassurance and a suggestion that we have a meditation on the Bible. Introducing this meditation I read the following passage from John 10, 7—9:

> *So Jesus spoke again: 'In truth, in very truth I tell you, I am the door of the sheepfold. The sheep paid no heed to anyone who came before me, for these were all thieves and robbers. I am the door; anyone who comes into the fold through me shall be safe. He shall go in and out and find pasturage.* (Emphasis my own)

She again started this meditation standing but sat down soon in a meditative position and put in front of herself, on a cushion, the drawing of herself with the outstretched hands at the wall in the empty room without windows and with a closed door. Soon I noticed that she breathed deeply—an indication that something had been touched in her. However, she remained silent during the whole exercise lasting one hour and then told me: "First I did not find

127

the door. Then the door was not far from me. Then I said' 'Jesus help me'. Then I was at the door like a lonely baby. I wanted to lie down, something in me said 'yes', something said 'no'. I enter into a struggle, a struggle between something in me that says: 'relax and trust' and a fear which says 'no' it is dangerous—a struggle between the deep 'me', who is small, hurting, who feels good in answering the inner voice that calls me to lie on the ground at the door and wait and the other 'me' who says . . . 'you don't lie on the ground, you don't do that, it won't give you anything. You—referring to me—are present. You can't do that in front of him.' The whole meditation was spent in this struggle and at the end I was getting more and more caught in the merry-go-round and was becoming more and more annoyed."

In the conversation which followed the sharing of this experience she recalled that when she was 4 years old she was standing at the door . . . indicating that "she could feel like standing at that door" wanting to go to her mother . . . but unable to move. I attempted to strengthen trust in her without going far into the fears evoked. I thought it would be best to wait and to do a 'lying down' exercise with her the next morning. We agreed to meet for a morning meditation, but she only came at 10 o'clock. She told me immediately that in the early morning she had had a profound experience. "I was awake at 5 o'clock, lying on my side in bed and the following words were running in my memory: 'Most of all, do not make any noise, He walks in the night, He walks close to you.' Jesus was seizing my whole being—like the eagle in the drawing of the dream I had twenty years ago. Little by little, I start feeling this presence but this time not only in my hands, as I often did before, but in my whole body. As it enters my body, it quiets me in a very forceful way. It penetrates like rays that go through me. The touch

128

produced is not one that reaches only the skin but one that touches through my body. When the quieting strong presence was in all my body, well established, I could not move. I remember desiring Jesus very vehemently and repeating continuously from something rising deep inside and in its mounting movement—calling Jesus, Jesus, Jesus . . ."

"The state of quieting was the most gentle total touch and the most powerful over me I ever experience. I realized I was in the position I resisted taking the day before during meditation (namely lying down) and I was most comfortable. It was where I should be. At one point one leg was numb and I was able to move it just a little and very slowly. I had the feeling I was under an anaesthetic. I felt time was passing. I did not lose the notion of it but it was not important to know exactly what time it was." These words speak for themselves. She was literally grasped by the presence of Jesus who "seized (her) whole being" yet left her with a deep longing. She could let herself go—lying down in trust—having been opened to the inflow, "the penetration" of a deeper reality of life.

After this experience,— which she insisted was "a visitation, was not of my initiative, it happened completely outside of my control"—she had to lie down in the afternoon: "My body needed to stay quiet, to rest, and only after three hours did I feel out of it and I felt a great hunger and newness and that I was back to normal."

As just mentioned this experience reminded her of a dream which she had about twenty years ago. The drawing of this dream showed her lying between two trees at winter time, her feet and her head touching the ground and her body bent, forming a half circle. Above her was an enormous eagle whose head was close to the crown

129

of the trees and whose claws were slightly above the highest point of her bent body while the two wings touched her head and her legs. She commented on this drawing:

"Beautiful, tall, majestic maple trees stood around a lawn in front of a school where I taught and lived. Many times daily I would stop and look at this scenery. Its beauty in each season I have admired in silence so many times and I was always renewed through this sight. Space, Peace, harmony, strength and life were messages coming to me through these short meditations. These are the surroundings where my dream took place. I remember clearly the descent of the eagle over me exactly in this setting. It was something like the visitation. The eagle was directly descending over me—it had the power of love. There was a strong sense of "you are precious to me—I want you for my own. I want all of you . . . The whole dream was like a very personal encounter with Jesus who was saying: 'You are mine' and was making me his by his touch. Afterwards I often wondered whether I was awake or asleep when this happened. I was twenty years old and this very personalized call and love of God for me was at the core of my decision to be a religious."

The parallelism between these two "visitations" is striking. The eagle is a symbol of light, renewal and transformation. The wings of the eagle do not only symbolize strength but also intuitional and spiritual potentiality (Exodus 19, 4; Isaiah 40, 31; C.G. Yung, *Collected Works*, vol. 12, p. 193). The eagle, symbol of the height and the sun, brought to her the love of Jesus, touching her innermost being. The first visitation was decisive for her becoming a nun, the second for freeing her to live her deepest commitment in a new way.

VI.

The next day Ruth asked me all kinds of questions with which I did not deal at great length because I felt it would not help her. I suggested instead a meditative exercise, asking her to search how she could relate the healing power which came alive in her the previous day to her wound, to what is not free in her.

She lay down, closed her eyes and spoke intermittently: "I feel comfortable . . . I feel warm . . . I feel good . . ." I suggested then she meet the lonely baby. Her response, after some time, was "I am stuck." I responded to this by suggesting "to contemplate . . . to look at the baby with her inner eye." Her first response was to move closer towards me (I was sitting next to her on the floor) saying "I am dependent". I said: "Yes, you are to be able to experience now the lonely baby." After some time she said: "it hurts . . . a big cut . . ." Sensing what was happening in her, namely a real experience of the wound, I gave her one hand and put my other hand on her head. She took my hand saying "light comes in." Then she cried, saying "I can feel the wound again." Later she described her feelings, saying "I cried like a child, a suffering child. I saw a long wound and felt the hurt of it. But I felt I must remain in that position. I felt pain but I felt comfortable, your presence was essential."

After this experience she drew "My wound". The drawing—which was different from the drawing she did at the very beginning, yet had similarities with it—consisted of a thin red line which stretched almost diagonally toward the top right hand corner of the paper. The central two-thirds of the line was thickened with a dark red surmounted by an undulating bright red mass as if formed by the gentle waves of the ocean. It was a deep wound, the dark red could have been clotted blood, the light red was like fresh blood untouched by time. "I was going slowly, drawing the wound" she reflected later "for it was painful. When I first started I burst out crying. Long sobs breaking out loud from deep within in a rapid succession decreasing in loudness with a decreasing amount of air in one breath. Four times I stopped drawing, for it was too painful. Four times I let my head fall on my hands on the table and cried desperately—it seemed the sound of my pain filled the house, the empty house, reaching each wall, touching each wall in the place."

The ability to descend into the wound, feeling and expressing the hurt at the same time as knowing that the cosmic forces inflicting the wound and threatening the very ground of her being can be mastered in a living trusting human relationship to another person constituted a decisive turning point in her quest to be free. In order to be able to move from the relatively un-emotional represented in her first drawing of "My wound" to such an experience of pain and renewal, she had to know that there is a love stronger than the forces inflicting the wound and she had to experience this ultimately deeper love in the reality of a human relationship. This experience was reflected in her thoughts about the day and the shared evening prayer: "Fred loves me—Jesus loves me. I sense that my wound must be surrounded by light but I can't put light around it on my drawing." For an experience of light which would not have been an artificial addition to her drawing of the wound she had to wait for the next day.

In the meantime she did another drawing—she drew herself in the room which she had drawn before but this time she was not alone in this room. There was a person facing her. There also was a window in the room. Her comments were: "I was touching this wound but I was not

132

alone. The door was no longer important. I felt like adding a window." Though drawn in the same earth colour as her first drawing of the room, the proportions of the room were quite different from those in her first drawing. There, the floor had stretched out—accentuated by her ourstretched arms—as if moving towards infinity. Everything was bare. The second drawing conveyed the feeling of a room in which one could live. The floor was grounded, surrounded by high walls. The window and the door were drawn in perspective, and there was life, symbolized by moving lines, on the floor. In its centre were two figures. The one whom she said represented me was in fact a man with a long flowing beard (I do not have a beard). This indicates that through our personal relationship she touched a transpersonal reality of the wise old man, of the healer. The way she drew herself had an embryonic quality. This expressed the redemption of the wounded baby. The way was opened for a rebirth. For her Jesus' words thus became a reality: "in truth, in very truth I tell you, unless a man has been born over again he cannot see the kingdom of God." (John 3, 4).

VII.

Ruth's final experience before parting after a week of common search was to enter the heart of Jesus. When she came for our last morning meditation she said: "I see the opened heart of Jesus and I recognize that the opening is the one I drew yesterday as my wound." She was surprised that she did not remember the heart of Jesus the day before when she was looking at her wound and felt that she had now "found her place". She described her meditative experience in these words: "I go into a rest gradually deeper. I hear a voice inside: Fred loves me, Jesus loves me. Then I see my heart around my wound and against the heart of Jesus—wound against wound. Warmth, peace, comfort—the only place where I can place my wounded heart. I could not draw light around my wound but now I am close to the light of the heart of Jesus."

Before we started the final meditation, she did a drawing showing her wound in the heart of Jesus. After she had done this, she became aware "of my desire when I am close to people—in love—to enter their heart. And now I feel like invited—wanting to go inside the door, inside the wound of Jesus' heart—which I do—the desire coincides with its realization. So I find my heart inside the heart of Jesus completely with light, warmth, well-being, surprised that I did not go there before. I remain there."

This experience was an intimately personal expression of the words which I had chosen for this meditation—the last before her departure:

I am the real vine, and my Father is the gardener. Every barren branch of mine he cuts away; and every fruiting branch he cleans, to make it more fruitful still. You have already been cleansed by the word that I spoke to you. Dwell in me, as I in you . . . (John 15, 1–3)

During this first week of our intensive encounter she experienced a whole cycle of redemption which opened a new vista for her. Now she had to relive this experience in its various phases at ever deeper levels to become truly free. Returning to her home country she took on new responsibilities in her work. Subsequently she had some intermittent help in exploring certain aspects of her inner journey and after two years returned to work through the deepest layers of her wound whose depth was already revealed but which was not healed in a way which gave her

134

back the energy she needed to build a new life for herself.

The freedom to do so became a reality two years later when she was ready to venture into a new direction, developing and living those potentialities which she had not been free to actualize so far.

VIII.

The day after her departure Ruth wrote: "I constantly go freely in and out of the heart. I am allowed and welcomed in. I'm always in but when I am aware of it, it's like entering again." With these words she expressed both the lasting reality of her experience and the continuous need for renewal. The wider significance of what happened to her may be summed up in three propositions: (1) it confirms the essential nature of the healing process as I observed it in my work as an analytical psychologist; (2) it illustrates my attempts to integrate systematically different approaches to healing, particularly as regards spiritual and psychological insights while being clearly centred and grounded in a deeper reality of life; it thus opens new vistas for more effective ways of fostering the healing process than any single one of the approaches used may have done on their own; and (3) being integrative in the sense just mentioned, a way is opened for a "new" wholeness, for a growth and development which enables us to actualize the potentialities of the new mode of consciousness whose dawn we are witnessing today.

As regards the essential nature of the healing process, the basic movement of change described here shows an interaction between the awakening of the light of counsciousness and the ability to descend into the darkness and thus to deprive it of its inhibiting power. This process can be observed at each stage of development: as new life is awakened, Ruth is able—and obliged—to face her wound more and more deeply.

This process is a complex one in which the source of healing and the source of injury interact. The former is a transpersonal reality and power which Ruth experiences most vividly through her intimate personal relationship with Jesus. The latter is also nourished by transpersonal forces—cosmic forces of evil. The latter can only be overcome because and inasmuch as the forces of light are ultimately stronger than the forces of darkness. To be human means to have to struggle so that light and love can predominate. Ruth's struggle between the desire to lie down in trust and to sit up in fear is but one illustration of this situation.

But the healing process is not merely a struggle. It is also participation in the quiet and usually slow movement of a spiritual fire alive in us and in the universe—the universal ground of life to which we referred repeatedly in Chapter 1. Ruth experienced it as "slow cooking". The way in which this fire can warm us and dissolve the congealed coldness hidden in the wound depends upon the nature and strength of the blockage which accompanies every wound. In the extreme case our access to the source of healing may be so blocked that only a relatively long process of recovery is possible. Ruth was more fortunate because she was never so cut off from the source of healing as to be unable to grow and develop. Granted she was repeatedly "stuck"—as she also was in our common search. But beyond this "stuckness" she always found the reality of Jesus, whether immediately present or whether his Presence was known to her in spite of its seeming absence.

In my encounters with people who are blocked in their development I have found as many types of relationships between the source of healing and the source of injury as I have met people. The specific approach must therefore be different in each situation. Yet common is the need to activate the healing power in a living relationship to a human being who "knows" and "loves" the wounded person. I put these words in quotation marks to indicate that the quality of this knowledge and love is different from the way these words are often used in everyday language, as indicated in Chapters 1 and 4. Though the events described here show clearly the fundamental role of a reality which is truly transpersonal—the visitations which Ruth experienced are a powerful example—only in exceptional situations can a deep wound be healed without a living relationship to another human being. It is true that this relationship must go deeper than what is usually called, in psychological jargon, "the transference" as the essay on "The Wounded Healer" which led to the encounter with Ruth, clearly shows.

Also of universal significance is the role of the will and of an inner attitude which has deeper roots than the energies expressed in our will-power yet which nourishes the latter. Ruth said rightly that the forces she has to encounter are stronger than those which she can muster with her will-power. However this does not mean that the will is unimportant. Quite to the contrary, it is very important in our determination to go in a certain direction even if we need transpersonal help to complete our journey. For Ruth will-power and the deep inner desire to live her life in harmony and union with Jesus became one. This enabled her to strive from the depth of her being to become free, thus uniting her will with a creative energy rooted in a deeper reality of life.

At the same time Ruth accepted her injury without resentment. We are touching here an ultimate mystery of the healing process—an inner attitude which enables us to say "yes" to our destiny—whatever this may be. This attitude is expressed in a "yes" to the wound rather than resentment when asking the unanswerable question "Why did this happen to me?" Such an acceptance combined with a deeply rooted determination to overcome the injury makes it possible to activate the light and love which alone can heal the wound. Ultimately, such an attitude opens us to the power of grace. Ruth could experience this power most deeply because she had the kind of acceptance and openness which enabled her to say "Your grace is enough for me."

IX.

The central significance of the spiritual quest in Ruth's experience does not need any further emphasis. It also was the core of the integration of different approaches which characterized my work with her.

Meditation—already mentioned in Chapter 1—played a central role in our work together. As the description of events showed I used different meditative approaches: silent meditation akin to contemplative prayer, meditation on a biblical text and a kind of meditation with which I became familiar in India and which has been systematically developed in Laya-Yoga. Yet all meditation, no matter what form it may take and in what tradition it may have been developed, touches a universal reality—otherwise it is not true meditation. There is, however, a fundamental difference between the way meditation has been traditionally used in Eastern religions and the kind of meditation which I consider most appropriate for an experience rooted in the Judeo-Christian tradition.

In order to understand this difference it is helpful to divide meditation into two stages. The first stage has the purpose of reaching a deeper reality of life, penetrating beyond the emotions and thoughts of daily life to that inner core where our true uniqueness merges with a universal power and truth. Essentially this signifies penetrating to the core of our own true self. The particular approach used in this first stage seems to me to be a matter of personal choice depending upon personal circumstances. The general distinction between meditative methods based on concentration on specific experiences or aspects of life on the one hand and methods aiming to empty ourselves on the other hand does not invalidate such a position since the ultimate objective of these opposite approaches is in fact the same, namely to enable us to penetrate to a deeper reality of life.

The difference between the "Eastern" tradition of meditation and the way I used it with Ruth becomes vital in the way the insights thus gained are used. If they are used in order to leave the world and its suffering and conflicts behind us by becoming one with a transcendental reality we remain in the Eastern tradition. However if, once we have reached this deeper reality of life, we enter a second stage, namely using these insights and the energy of transformation activated in the process, in *order* to be able to transform our *whole* personality — including our daily relationships to people, the human community, society, nature etc. — then we are using meditative exercises to develop a spirit-centred mode of consciousness encompassing the totality of our life experience.

This is the way I used the meditative exercises with Ruth. Spiritual insights and energy were not only used for transformation of the inner world—including what we usually call the psyche, but soul and psyche, spiritual and psychological insights were interrelated in the meditative process form the very beginning. This was partly achieved by the way the meditative exercises were used, partly by relating the meditation on a biblical text directly to a problematic psychological situation—as for example in the meditation on Jesus as the door when Ruth found herself in a room whose door was closed.

In my exploration with Ruth I did not make any attempt to work with the energy centres. This was partly due to the fact that I knew we would be separated after a week by great distance and I did not want to activate energies with which she might be unable to deal on her own. Partly it was because I knew that Ruth was already open to these energies. The sensitivity in her hands and the sensitivity of her whole body—as manifested in her experience in the mountains and in what she described as visitations—were in fact expressions of an open relationship to these centres.

I am fully aware that there are a number of complementary modes of healing which are important if we want to move towards a truly holistic approach. We are in the process of including these in the development of such an approach in the New Era Centre. The work with Ruth was centred in the Spirit and characterized by an integration of the spiritual and the psychological. There is indeed an inner connection between Ruth's experience and what St. John of the Cross called "the dark night of the soul": darkness experienced in the innermost knowledge of the presence of God. "Open to the gift of the moment with all my heart", Ruth knew in this "moment" a timeless presence though it was still night. It was a time of expectant waiting, preparatory to "the coming of Jesus" who brings light and love and whose coming, though in the future, is already experienced in that moment which constitutes the Eternal Now.

The light which makes it possible to face this darkness is leading us, as we have already mentioned, to a growing discovery of darkness. The lights opens our eyes and enables us to see aspects of our life hitherto hidden from us. It often reveals a pain which we could not face until light and love made it possible to open ourselves to the healing forces as well as to the darkness in our soul. The light which makes this possible has a universal quality. When Jesus said "I am the Light of the World", he referred to this light. He spoke as a Jew of the reality of the universal cosmic Christ alive in him. He did not speak as a secretarian Christian. This is important because the universal reality of Christ manifests itself in infinite personally unique forms and in manifold culturally conditioned ways. Unless this situation is deeply respected, we violate the integrity of a person and fail to activate the healing power of transformation of the universal cosmic Christ. In Ruth's experience Jesus of Nazareth was the Christ with whom she had a personally central and living experience. In a Jewish girl with whom I worked, this reality came alive in the experience of the fish—symbol of a deeper reality of life accepted by the early Christians as a symbol of their experience of Jesus as the Christ.

Without pretending that we have an ultimate judgment, there is a strong presumption that an approach combining various methods has a reasonable chance to be more effective than a limitation to any one method. But we must be careful not to generalize from the limited experience we have so far. A great deal more in-search and

141

research is imperative to help us understand the interaction of various approaches and make us ever more
effective in helping the power of the Spirit to come alive.

X.

No matter what the answer will be to the question of
effectiveness—and I am sure that it will differ according
to different individual personal situations—there is no
doubt about the appropriateness, even necessity of an
integrative approach in order to develop the new wholeness which has become a potential of our time.

The striving for wholeness is not new. Indeed it is as
old as humankind. But each personal situation, each stage
in the development of consciousness opens new potentialities for wholeness which did not exist in other situations
and at other times—or which existed only for those exceptional people whom we call saintly. The new consciousness opens potentialities for integrating what we
usually call the psychological, the spiritual and the com-
munal-societal in ways which did not exist for most people
at earlier stages of the evolutionary process. Previously
we did not have the kind of knowledge of deeper psychospiritual processes which the development of depth psychology, of clinical theology and of the sociology of
knowledge is now giving us.

In concluding, I want to emphasize that the new unity
of the spiritual, psychological and societal is clearly
reflected in a renewed understanding of the true self. The
latter unites our relationships to ourselves, to our fellow
human beings, to the human community, to organized
society, to nature and to a deeper reality of life. The

unity of the true self is a wholeness which brings the different aspects of our being and the different spheres of life into the harmony of a new era.

EPILOGUE

As we are entering a new era in the development of human consciousness and the corresponding human community, new vistas in healing are opening up. Health and healing are finding a more wholistic expression. At the same time we are becoming more conscious of the partiality and conditioning of all human insight. Yet this very recognition is opening wider horizons since it is the result of a greater consciousness of the universal ground of all life.

The new awareness finds its deepest expression in a striving to build the New Jerusalem. We find the building stones for such an endeavour as we go to the roots of our heritage becoming at the same time citizens of the planet earth. This is indeed the expression of our ability to share the true essence of our humanity in the spirit of the new era. As we commit ourselves to such an endeavour we touch those deepest springs of health which open us to the mystery of our embeddedness in the Divine.

The New Era Centre at The Abbey in Sutton Courtenay

The Abbey is the home of a community who seek to rediscover the way of Christ in the context of today.

OUR GOAL is to bring the spiritual, the psychological and the social into a unity so that the Spirit may become the Centre, illuminating all life.

OUR PURPOSE is that the timeless reality of Christ's New Era be recognised and experienced in the new era of human history which is now emerging.

We therefore co-operate with the universal truth by offering opportunities for personal growth, for social transformation and for ecological living.

We also celebrate this truth in worship, art, research, writing and the whole of life.

OUR PROGRAMME provides a wide range of opportunities to meet, to reflect and to work together on an ecumenical inter-faith basis. A wide range of events is planned each year, both residential and non-residential, and open to anyone interested in sharing our explorations.

Events include day, weekend and longer workshops, conferences, seminars and retreats; evening talks and lecture series; exhibition, concerts, arts and crafts classes, art workshops and other related events; opportunities to explore personal growth within the perspectives of depth psychology and spiritual direction.

OUR SETTING is a beautiful quadrangular stone building with an enclosed courtyard, dating from the early fourteenth century, with a large mediaeval hall. Outbuildings in the wooded grounds provide art and craft workshops and modern accommodation for small residential groups. The Abbey is located on the village green in the Thames-side village of Sutton Courtenay in South Oxfordshire.

Information about the Centre is available from The Abbey, Sutton Courtenay, Abingdon, OX14 4AF, England

A DAY AT A TIME
by
Denis Duncan

A thought and a prayer for
each day of a year

ARTHUR JAMES
One Cranbourne Road,
London N10 2BT

Ninety-minute audio cassettes
of
WILLIAM BARCLAY and J B PHILLIPS

are available through Arthur James Limited

WILLIAM BARCLAY gives expositions of
The Lord's Prayer and The Beatitudes

J B PHILLIPS speaks on
When God Was Man and A Translator's Experience

Arthur James Limited also publishes the following books by
WILLIAM BARCLAY

THE NEW TESTAMENT: A Translation
with introductions to each book and notes on difficult passages
available in both Hardback and Paperback editions

THE MIND OF JESUS — an exposition of Jesus' teaching

CRUCIFIED AND CROWNED — the great events of Jesus' last days

THROUGH THE YEAR WITH WILLIAM BARCLAY

EVERY DAY WITH WILLIAM BARCLAY

MARCHING ORDERS and MARCHING ON
for younger people

Also available through Arthur James Limited is
SEVEN FRESH WINESKINS — an exposition of
Old Testament passages

and by J B PHILLIPS
THROUGH THE YEAR WITH J B PHILLIPS

For the full list of books on healing, prayer, pastoral ministry, etc.,
write to
ARTHUR JAMES LIMITED
One Cranbourne Road, London N10 2BT